# Turn it Down!

## Songs, Stories, and Other Spiritual Stuff

CW00952261

davehopwood.com

For Simeon Wood.

This is all your fault.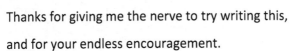

Thanks for giving me the nerve to try writing this,

and for your endless encouragement.

**Sunshine on a Cloudy Day**

In the film *Music and Lyrics* Alex Fletcher, played by Hugh Grant, comes up with this great quote about pop songs. He says that any line from all the great novels in the world cannot make you feel anything like as good, in such a short space of time, as a line from The Temptations' *My Girl*. A song which describes sunshine on a day full of clouds, and warmth on a chilly cold day. And all to an endorphin-busting tune. He then lists a few great songwriters, those who bring such life-infused tunes into our lives. Smokey Robinson, Stevie Wonder, Bob Dylan, The Beatles.

That's me. That's my take on it too. These poets can not only make us feel good, they move us, they fire us up, they calm us down, they enrage us, they motivate us and they inspire us. In just three minutes. That is something.

**Fraud**

We artists, and I use the word verrrrry loosely with regard to myself, fear being found out, unmasked as frauds, not as smart or special as people think. Perhaps we inadvertently set ourselves on a pedestal, legends in our own mind, capable of changing the universe one song, one line, one picture, one book, one tune, one performance at a time. So I'm unmasking myself here, disclosing myself as a true fraud. To misquote Julia Roberts in *Notting Hill,* 'I'm just a guy, here in front of you, with a handful of thoughts, asking you to go easy on me.' And when it comes to improving the universe I try and hold on to a simpler thought, changing the world one smile at a time.

### Boogieing

I've never been a discerning or sophisticated listener, I just fall for whatever grabs my ear-gear and sneaks into my head. I have huge gaps in my knowledge too. I know little or nothing about Pink Floyd, or Led Zeppelin, or Deep Purple, or prog rock, or hip hop, or heavy metal, or emo, or Gilbert and Sullivan, or Mantovani, or opera, or Flanders and Swan, or classical. I'm tempted to label myself a Philistine at this point, but I believe the Philistines were actually rather cultured. So I guess, I'm just me. 😊

I have just been listening to a programme about the brilliant guitarist Jeff Beck, who was endlessly creative with the sounds he made, but I realise I know him best for the infectious *Hi Ho Silver Lining* and not least for the version recently done by Imelda May for the second *Fisherman's Friends* movie. I tend to like what I like and often keep quiet about the cheesier end of that. (Not in this book though!) Over the years I have acquired albums by everyone from Magazine to The Nolans, Showaddywaddy to Stiff Little Fingers, The Carpenters to The Clash, John Barry to Cliff Richard.

My love for pop music began early, I was born in 1962, the year The Beatles had their first hit. I missed their reign, and only caught up later. Same with The Kinks, and much of The Who, The Rolling Stones, Manfred Mann and so many others. I did buy my first single in the '60s, but the '70s was really my era. I left the hit parade behind for much of the '80s, and picked things up again in the '90s, though it was becoming a love/hate thing by then. The new century has been hit and miss for me. I want to be 'down with the kids', but let's be honest, these days if I could get down with anyone, it's unlikely I'd get back up again.

### Doors

I don't play a musical instrument. I started learning the guitar at eighteen but then I saw a mime artist, Geoffrey Stevenson and drama took over my focus and energy. I picked up my daughter's ukulele in the 2020 lockdown and found a lesson on YouTube, but soon I was making videos for online church services and other projects took over.

I worked in a bank from 1979 to 1984 and they used to pay us profit sharing each January, so one year I bought a small keyboard. But the mechanics and digital dexterity were beyond me. My fingers wouldn't do the walking. They tripped over themselves or meandered off course. Listening and dancing to and thinking about songs is my limit.

So any opinions I have don't come from a place of technique or ability, just from a cave of my own ideas. And is dependent on which sounds have made their way into my ears and shoved open the doors of my heart.

### Oops

I've always found happy, catchy tunes uplifting, those most easy on the ears, and I feel I should apologise for liking songs by Showaddywaddy, The Carpenters, Abba, The Nolans, S Club 7. Because many of them are, well, seen as a little bit naff and commercial, and I am not *supposed* to like them.

Mind you The Beautiful South did a great album of diverse covers, *Golddiggas, Headnodders & Pholk Songs*, on which they did a version of S Club 7's *Don't Stop Moving* so they must have liked them too. The album also features such classics as *Don't Fear the Reaper* and *You're the One That I Want,* both done in that inimitable Beautiful South way.

I could try and present the case that, once in a blue moon, I have wished I was passionate about some other music, as pop is considered such a lowbrow art form. But I don't think that's true. Though I may have appeared embarrassed sometimes when confessing my fondness for the top forty. I'm me and this is who I am, why try to be something else? I'd be a shark trying to ride a unicycle, wouldn't I. So as I sit and write this I'm not convinced that I have ever really wanted to escape my love of pop.

### Hep

At the other end of the hep spectrum I also feel I should apologise for not liking rap and hip hop. I confess I am behind the times here. It's a dominant genre now. So popular, and with plenty to say. In my defence I do like one or two, The Black Eyed Peas' *Where's the Love* comes to mind, and there's a good message in that one as well. Less of a good message in House of Pain's *Jump Around* but that's a favourite an' all.

8

I believe rap made its first insurgence into the mainstream with The Sugarhill Gang and *Rapper's Delight*, and The Gap Band's *Oops, Up Side Your Head*. A.k.a. *The Rowing Song* due to the sit-down-and-do-some-rowing-on-the-floor dance that we all did to it. I have to confess to liking that one too, and was more than happy to throw myself down and bust a few rowing moves.

### Top Fives

Being a chart fan I couldn't resist including numerous random Top Five listings, and many of them contain more than five songs. (There are three kinds of mathematicians in the world, those who can do maths and those who can't.) I should also say any references in the book to chart placings refers to the UK hit parade. Some of my top five listings appear with a logical connection to what has gone before, some don't. Bird Songs for example. No real reason for that to be in here. That was just a topic that popped into my head so I included it. Good job Terrifying Villains didn't pop into my head instead or you'd have had Bony M's *Ma Baker,* Georgie Fame's *The Ballad of Bonnie and Clyde, The Phony King of England* (from Disney's Robin Hood)... and *Mr Blobby*. I'll stop there.

### Ghost Story

When I was at junior school we used to tell a ghost story. It went something like this.

We were walking along the moor one night, there was Fred and Joe and me. We came to a big old house. Fred went inside… and didn't come out. Joe went inside… and didn't come out. Then I went inside. One year later Fred went mad. Two years later Joe went mad. And it's exactly three years ago today since it happened to…. MEEEEEEEEEEEEEEE!!!! At which point we howled the last word, hoping to make the listening crowd jump out of their skin. Even if they had heard it before.

I think of that tale sometimes when I hear the classic *Hotel California* by the Eagles. It's one of the great story songs, about a guy who gets weary while travelling and has to stop for the night. He finds this eerie place, full of whispers and strangers. The Hotel California. It always reminds me of Fred and Joe and me going mad in that house on the moor. (I'm better now.)

### Top Five Favourite Story Songs
*Hotel California* (The Eagles)
*Goodnight Saigon* (Billy Joel)
*American Pie* (Don McLean)
*Wuthering Heights* (Kate Bush)
*Park Life* (Blur)

### Catchy Numbers
I think I mentioned that I'm a sucker for a catchy tune. I've just been watching a documentary about New York's Brill Building, a thriving hit factory in the '50s and '60s, where groups of talented artists produced hit after hit. The likes of Neil Sedaka and Carole King scribbled catchy number after catchy number so that the hip singers and groups of their day could fill the airwaves with hooky three-minute tunes. When Dire Straits sang

about *Romeo and Juliet* back in 1980 they made reference to a Brill classic with the line about Juliet being under Romeo's window singing a line about her boyfriend being back. I thought she was just waxing lyrical about Romeo, but it seems now she was also quoting the Angels from 1963.

I come to so many of these songs late, but the easy-on-the-ears nature means I'm instantly grabbed. Bruce Springsteen's latest album is a collection of Northern Soul classics. The Boss cranking out a load of tunes from the sweaty dance halls of the '60s, no doubt packed with memories for him. I discovered Northern Soul late via an online documentary. Young adults spinning and twisting all weekend in northern UK dance halls to rediscovered American soul classics. I could spend my life watching programmes like this, the university of life just keeps on giving. And when I find one of my daughters playing a song I used to love I feel I'm helping complete their education in some way.

### Beginnings

There was no Northern Soul in our house in the early 70s though. Instead we had a clutch of novelty singles. *Ernie* by Benny Hill, complete with the classic B-side *Ting-A-Ling-A-Loo*, Middle of the Road's *Chirpy Chirpy Cheep Cheep*, and not forgetting The Scaffold's *Lily the Pink*. Ah, Lily the Pink. I knew all the words about Jennifer Eccles and her terrible freckles. And I found it to be a rather haunting tale, as it ended with dear Lily going up to heaven. The theology was okay, (although I feel the need to point out she wasn't actually the saviour of the human race, for that I suggest taking a gander at the gospel of Mark), but it seemed such a shame the pink one had to leave. I believe the song was number one in the hit parade for four weeks. And the band includes the famous Mike McGear – yes! Only the younger brother of one Paul McCartney. Forget *Penny Lane*, Lily's the thing. 😊

I've just discovered that Lily the Pink is actually based on an old folk song called *The Ballad of Lydia Pinkham*. Lydia was a real person, famous for inventing a tonic for menstrual and menopausal problems. Who knew? Well, The Shenanigans for sure, as you can see them singing it on YouTube. But back to those early records. The first single I remember going out to buy was *The Legend of Xanadu* by Dave Dee, Dozy, Beaky, Mick and Tich. A band who were extremely successful for a time, it's said that between 1965 and 1969 they spent more weeks on the chart than The Beatles. They only had one number one though (a little shy of the seventeen that The Beatles managed). And that was the one I bought, hopefully I had a certain influence on their success. It was 1968 and I was just five.

I recall Dave Dee cracking a whip on Top of the Pops as he sang, that must have been worrying for the camera crew. And maybe it sowed the seeds in my psyche for my later dedication to Indiana Jones. I have half an idea that also I went out to buy *Sugar Sugar* by The Archies at some point. But I might be imagining that. I don't think I got it anyway. Probably sold out. I've always loved that Tate and Lyle number, a song that was originally offered to The Monkees, who turned it down as they wanted to move into a more serious musical phase. Bit of a mistake as it went on to be the biggest selling single of the year. Oh well. The Archies weren't actually a real band. They were a fictional cartoon group, although some might suggest that of The Monkees too. 😊

Some space for any thoughts, doodlings, scribblings, top fives, or musical memories of your own.

**115**

No idea what my second purchase was, I didn't buy many singles back then. I often strummed through my parents' collection of LPs – they had *South Pacific*, and *The Sound of Music* (I think everybody had those two), and also possibly *West Side Story*. The *South Pacific* soundtrack was, believe it or not, number one in the album chart for... are you sitting down... sixty, yes – sixty weeks. And that was just in the 1950s. In the 1960s it clocked up another fifty-five, making one hundred and fifteen weeks at number one. I kid you not. And we thought Bryan Adams was outstaying his welcome with that Robin Hood number.

My mum and dad also had other albums, including Simon and Garfunkel's greatest hits. Plus an old disc of the sound of someone driving a tractor. Really. I don't think I'm misremembering that. It may have been a vinyl 78. I say vinyl, everything was on vinyl. We could only dream of TDK cassettes getting tangled round the heads of your tape player. Those heady spooling days were light years away. Paul and Art's greatest hits collection was the fourth biggest seller of the 1970s, they weren't the biggest LP because that was their other little record *Bridge Over Troubled Water*.

### Love and War

The LP I played over and over was *Geoff Love's Big War Movie Themes*. Now *that* was an album. Love and War you might say. I loved it. The disc was jammed with those themes from *The Great Escape, Bridge Over the River Kwai, The Dambusters, The Battle of Britain, The*

*Longest Day, 633 Squadron, The Guns of Navarone* and *Where Eagles Dare*. Not only had I seen most of the films, but the tunes were memorable, hummable numbers too. Not all though. *Lawrence of Arabia* was hard to whistle, and I'd never heard of *Is Paris Burning?* And haven't seen it to this day. I've just looked up Mr Love only to find he also did a ton of albums under the guise of Manuel and his Music of the Mountains. I recall he had a hit with *Rodrigo's Guitar Concerto* in 1976, but I never knew Manuel and Geoff were one and the same! (What would we do without Wikipedia eh?)

I used to play the *Big War Movie Themes* in our lounge in Cornwall on our Dansette record player, it was mounted in a solid blue box big enough and strong enough to sit on. When you were seven anyway. I played that disc over and over. Knew the album back to front. The cover was great too with its technicolour sketch of John Wayne, Peter O'Toole and some other fella. With the bridge exploding over the River Kwai in the background. I must have stared at that thing for hours. Back then you could digest such things like that.

That was the wonder of records, they came with covers and sleeves and that vinyl smell. We had a special oblong duster you could hold onto the record as it went round. Not as you were playing it though, that was the quickest way to the scourge of vinyl. Scratching. And I don't mean like those hip happening DJs do now. These scratches meant you could be stuck in the middle of track three forever. Crackle click crackle click crackle click crackle click crackle click... I'm assured by Wikipedia that Geoff Love released his war opus in

1971. Perfect timing then for moving on to the music of my sister.

**Top Five War Themes**
*A Bridge Too Far*
*The Great Escape*
*633 Squadron*
*Memphis Belle (Danny Boy)*
*Bridge Over the River Kwai*

**Feathercuts**
I don't mean that my sister actually recorded any songs, she was only about thirteen then. But Donny and David were on the scene. Yes. Osmond and Cassidy. *Puppy Love* and *Daydreamer*. Ah, those heartthrobs with their feather-cuts, wide lapels and flares. Bowie and Bolan were on the scene too, and I remember liking *Space Oddity* and *Metal Guru*. Only later would I buy greatest hits collections and discover classics like *Starman* and *Ride a White Swan*.

The early '70s is a fuzzy period in my memory. I became aware of popular songs on the radio such as *When Will I See You Again, Rock Your Baby, Band of Gold, Miss Grace, I Can't Give You Anything But My Love.* But knowing exactly when I first heard them or if I was regularly listening to them is hard to say. I was aware of Slade too, as Marc Bolan faded and the boys from Birmingham grew popular. *Mama Weer All Crazee Now* comes to mind, and *Gudbuy T' Jane*. (Gudness mee, wheare dyd thees guyze lurn two spelle?) These songs and others seemed to be forever in the

17

background in the early 70s. And they bring back hazy and nostalgic memories of that time. That's the best I can say. Hard to be specific.

### Blitz

I recently read about the boys from the glam band The Sweet, and how they came up with their early 70s sound. They were playing a concert and not going down well at all. People started throwing things and there was chaos. However, instead of giving up, they went away and wrote *Ballroom Blitz*, a reimagining of that concert in which the larking of the audience threw a shedload of energy into the mix and turned the anarchic event into something of good order. And this defined the next few hits they scored. A great example of that old adage, if life gives you a lemon... make a bacon sandwich.

### Cover Up

I started going to Redruth Grammar school in 1974. You had to be careful about revealing your musical tastes at school. Didn't want to get caught out liking The Wombles or The Osmonds when you had the likes of Bowie and Rod Stewart around.

In the second form we used to listen to the chart on a Tuesday lunchtime. One of the class had a little transistor radio and on March 23rd 1976 we were listening to the new countdown in our classroom. We heard that Tina Charles had slipped from the top position down to number three, which left just two songs. I was a big fan of Billy Ocean, and I wearily announced that he must be number one with *Love*

*Really Hurts Without You*. In fact we soon discovered that Brotherhood of Man had begun their six-week reign at the top, after winning Eurovision.

The interesting thing is (you see, there is a purpose to this story) that I felt the need to pretend to be unhappy about the possibility of Mr Ocean being at number one. It was all cover up. I would have been secretly over the moon about that. As it was, in our house, Brotherhood of Man were also flavour of the month. But I couldn't show any of that. Life was often full of musical pretence. The peer pressure was immense, at least in my head anyway. That lunchtime was one of the many occasions when I was hiding my true self.

Something that continues to this day, at least with regard to my faith. I often feel I'm living a half-life, I go out in public and am hopeless at telling others I am a Christian. If you give me a microphone and an audience I'm fine. I'm very happy to talk about what I believe in that instance. But one to one, I fumble for words. I think I'm too concerned about upsetting others, challenging what they believe.

When I was part of a theatre company and we sometimes did outreach in the streets, I was as likely to end up asking those I met what they believed as much as coming clean about my worldview. I believe it passionately, it's in my DNA, but I'm like Mr Bean when relating to others in normal life. It may have something to do with having a writer's brain. When I write I'm constantly rearranging sentences and editing phrases. In a conversation you can't do that, when it's out there it's out there. And small talk is an uphill battle for me.

**Top Five Cheesy But Irresistible Songs (for me anyway)**
*Red Light Spells Danger* (Billy Ocean)
*Give Me What I Ask For* (Cliff Richard)
*Sugar Sugar* (The Archies)
*Your Kisses Sweet* (Syreeta)
*Sad Sweet Dreamer* (Sweet Sensation)

### Trivia

1976 was the year when I really woke up to music. I had a cassette recorder (Yay! Get your pencils ready for all that spooling) for my birthday and so could start to record the songs I loved – FOR KEEPS! Or till the cassette tape got caught in the heads anyway. *Bohemian Rhapsody* had been at number one over Christmas '75, and I recall sitting on the sofa and watching what is now dubbed the first ever pop video, as Freddy and his pals kaleidoscoped around the screen. *Mamma Mia* knocked them off the top, becoming Abba's chart-topping comeback and their second number one after 1974's *Waterloo*. In effect this was kickstarting their six years of colossal success. 1976 would see them have three number ones and one number three. As well as two massive-selling albums, *Greatest Hits* and *Arrival*.

That first greatest hits collection was odd in that it featured three number ones (*Waterloo, Mamma Mia* and *Fernando*), a number six (*SOS*), and a load of other catchy tracks that had never done much charting at all. And it went on to be the second biggest selling album of the 1970s! Behind Paul and Art's *Bridge Over Troubled etc.* A couple of odd and unnecessary facts about *Mamma Mia* and *Bohemian Rhapsody* – both titles went on to spawn huge movies, and both songs featured the phrase 'Mamma Mia'. So there. I'm nothing if not full of disposable trivia.

The charts do unexpected things too (I've really got my anorak on now), Joe Dolce's *Shaddap Your Face* kept the epic *Vienna* off the top in 1981, while in 1967 Engelbert Humperdinck's *Please Release Me* denied The Beatles a number one with *Strawberry Fields/Penny Lane*, surely one of the best double A-sides ever. And to think that *Yellow Submarine* topped the charts for four weeks! It did have *Eleanor Rigby* on the other side, so maybe that was part of its success. (I don't dislike the aforementioned ode to that submarine, not at all, but it's not up there with *Penny Lane* or *Strawberry Fields*.) *Don't Stop Me Now* is one of Queen's most popular tracks these days, yet it didn't even make the top ten in 1978. Enough trivia, I'll get my coat... oh no I've already got my anorak on. On we go...

### Total Eclipse of the Chart

Nowadays the charts have changed, with the advent of streaming they now measure what we listen to as much as what we buy. Back in my day songs tended to enter the chart low down, slowly climb to a peak and then drop, and in that sense they had a story to their rise and fall.

In the '90s that changed as singles started to enter the chart at their highest position, i.e. most people bought them on their week of first release, and after that they steadily dropped. Songs regularly went straight in at number one, something very rare in the '70s and '80s. It all got a bit boring really, and very few songs actually went up the charts.

Now, with the advent of streaming and downloading, songs do tend to climb again, plus at Christmas the listing fills with old festive favourites. Wham's *Last Christmas* and Mariah Carey's *All I Want for Christmas Is You* used to be famous for never having made number one, in the past few years they both have.

Oh and if you add this into the mix – a song that only remained at number one for two weeks in 1981 (Soft Cell's *Tainted Love*) could outsell a song that was at number one for five weeks the same year (Adam and the Ants' *Stand and Deliver*) – then it just goes to show the chart is far from an exact science. A song by Queen that failed to make the top ten – *Don't Stop Me Now* – proves to have far more longevity than one of their number one hits – *Innuendo.* For me this just adds to the fascination and strangeness of it all.

Mind you, it should be noted that the charts don't really exist anyway. Not in their own right as a 'thing'. They are merely a measuring device, a listing. All they do is reflect what is currently popular, so when I lament the passing of a particular era of chart activity, it's a pointless exercise really. The chart is not responsible for the behaviour of singles. It would be a bit like blaming the TV set for the programmes that get broadcast. That said, shouting at the telly can still feel like a worthwhile pastime.

And I realise I *still* have that chart anorak on. Back to those flared-trousered, chopper-biked '70s.

## The Goodies

The first thing I recorded on my brand-new cassette machine was not actually a song, but rather a Christmas episode of the Goodies. I'm a little hazy about when I got the recorder, but Christmas '75 seems to fit, so let's settle on that. I can always tweak it in a future edition of this book. The first cassette I had was only fifteen minutes a side, I discovered this when I tried to record the thirty-minute episode in one go and there was a click halfway through, followed by a repeated series of clicks as I persistently tried to hold down the record button without flipping the cassette. I could have just read the length of it on the cassette label, but hey-ho. I learnt the hard way.

I soon started buying C60s, C90s and C120s, also learning the hard way that two hours' worth of cassette tape doesn't always behave properly. Thank goodness they didn't make C240s. There'd have been unspooled tape everywhere. I also learned the hard way that handling unspooling tape with your fingers results in strange muffled and wowing sounds when you try and record on it again. Ho hum. Life is never straightforward. But record on it I did. In the summer holidays I sat with my recorder in the lounge beside my parents' big upright radio, when the house was quiet. That's a relative term of course because I was making a heck of a racket with the radio, it's just that there was no one else around to add background noise to my precious recording.

On certain days in the holidays I used to buy a packet of Crawfords Cheddars and sit by the radio for hours waiting for songs to record. I guess my mum and dad were out at work and my sister was in charge. Not sure if I ate anything else on those recording days, but the Cheddars went down a treat.

I'd perch on the edge of my seat, both physically and emotionally, pressing record whenever I caught the opening bars of my latest favourites, beneath the patter of such DJs as Tony Blackburn, 'Diddy' David Hamilton, and Johnny Walker. And then all the way through I'd be clenching everything hoping that they'd play the song in its entirety and not interrupt it with some unnecessary comment before the song ended or faded completely.

Of course they inevitably did. They didn't want punters like me making pristine recordings and selling them in the local market I guess. I didn't ever sell them, they were too precious to me. I did once record a whole three-hour Tony Blackburn show for my sister, she was off on a school trip and wanted something her class could listen to on the coach.

### Killing and Thieves

From 1970 to 1977 we lived in Alexandra Close, in a little Cornish village called Illogan. I had a group of friends in the close, and we indulged in all the frenetic and chaotic games that suited our age. We played in the road and in each other's gardens; killing each other was popular, as we re-enacted World War Two. I also made up scratch plays that we performed to long-suffering family members. I wasn't good at sport but we kicked a ball around and did our best to avoid the cars. And we hurled ourselves at one another in games like British

Bulldog. But at times I would retreat into my own world. I collected and painted Airfix models and soldiers, and also wanted to write stories and so was trying to do that. I often got frustrated that it took so long. I wanted the idea on the page as soon as it crept into my head.

I learned about the need for tension and suspense when I wrote a tale about some jewel thieves smuggling a precious gem out of the country. One of the gang created a fake flap of skin, stitched between his shoulder blades, and hid the diamond underneath it. The problem was they achieved it easily. They were too good! They managed the whole thing without a hitch and I had this sense that the story was dissatisfying. I also spent a lot of time recording off the radio, it was a dedicated hobby, and one that swallowed hours, days of my time. But I loved it and in some ways I was never happier than pressing record and watching that cassette spool round.

### Hello Muddah

We loved novelty records in our house. Things like *Hello Muddah, Hello Fadduh* (*The Camp Granada Song*) by Allan Sherman, *Right Said Fred* by Bernard Cribbins, and *My Brother* by Terry Scott. My sister once wrote in to Radio Two to request it for my birthday, on a Christmas Eve edition of Junior choice. The song got played but not her request, in some ways fortunate as I'd nipped to the loo just before Ed 'Stewpot' Stewart began reading out the dedications for it. I always did have impeccable timing.

Laurel and Hardy's revival of their *Trail of the Lonesome Pine* was another favourite, and my dad and I also loved *King of the Cops* by Billy Howard, a spoof of Roger Miller's fantastic *King of the Road*. We loved those TV detectives, the likes of Columbo, Ironside, Kojac and Cannon, so this was perfect, as it featured Billy Howard impersonating them all. I'm a sucker for impressions to this day. The Proclaimers did a great version of it too. *King of the Road* that is, not *King of the Cops*. I don't think they do impressions.

Some space for any thoughts, doodlings, scribblings, top fives, or musical memories of your own.

**A Christmas Top ~~Five~~ Eight**

*Great Big Sled* (The Killers)
*Santa Claus is Coming to Town* (Bruce Springsteen)
*Christmas in the Air (Tonight)* (Scouting for Girls)
*I Wish It Could be Christmas Every Day* (Wizzard)
*Merry Christmas, Happy New Year* (Ingrid Michaelson & Zooey Deschanel)
*Christmas Time* (The Darkness)
*We Built this City on Sausage Rolls* (LadBaby)
*Wombling Merry Christmas* (The Wombles) – I have to include it, it brings back such happy memories

**Float On**

We also had a few K-Tel compilation albums. K-Tel were the forerunners of the *Now That's What I Call Music* dynasty. Their 1976 album *Hit Machine* 'as advertised on TV' brought us twenty-two hits by twenty-two original stars. As opposed to the Top of the Pops albums which were all cover versions by unnamed musicians. We bought *Hit Machine* and I played it lots, it may have been mine or my sister's. Not sure. It featured the likes of Slik, Guys and Dolls, The Bay City Rollers and Mud.

We also had 1977's *Disco Fever*. That featured the number one single from The Floaters called *Float On*. A song which drove the young teen version of me mad as it featured all four members of the group introducing themselves and telling you what star sign they were and which kind of woman they would like. 'Hi, I'm Musgrove and I'm a piscesagidumpling and I like a woman who can sort out the economy, bring peace to the Middle East

28

and cut the lawn while she's at it.' I jest of course. There was no Musgrove. Not in The Floaters anyway.

My wife and I have just had a discussion about another 1976 epic *Disco Rocket*, we discovered in the late 90s we had **both** bought it as youngsters. Spooky. It's quite clear we were destined to be married. It had various hits of 1976 including *Let's Stick Together* by Bryan Ferry – an intriguing and brilliant reworking of Canned Heat's *Let's* Work *Together.* Canned Heat's original seems to have been about people coming together for the greater good. Mr Ferry took it and made it about rebuilding a struggling marriage. With a great saxophone on it too.

*Disco Rocket* also offered Sailor's *Girls Girls Girls*, not sure if the lyrics might be a tad less acceptable now (I find it hard to keep up), and David Dundas's Brutus advert song *Jeans On. Jeans On* has lived a long time in our household, when our older daughter Amy was young we played it a lot and often jumped around madly on the bed to it. It became a Hopwood favourite all over again.

### Call the Doctor

Tina Charles is also on this compilation with a lesser hit. She'd been at number one with *I Love to Love*, and I think this song, *Love Me Like a Lover* (as opposed to a traffic warden or a mime artist)*,* was a follow up. She had originally been in the group 5000 Volts (anyone remember *Dr Kiss Kiss* or *I'm On Fire*?) and went on to have several solo hits including one called *Dr Love*. I just reminded my wife it made number four in the charts.

That's the sort of pop nerd I am. There's something about the magic achievement of making the top five, I often remember whether a song managed to sneak inside it or not.

I never quite knew what Ms Charles was singing in the chorus on that one, and for years I got the lines wrong, thought she was asking for the doctor to 'love me somebody...' which really makes no sense, but it turns out she was actually asking for the doctor to come running, which probably would get a doctor on the scene (we're talking about the days before the NHS crisis).

And on the subject of misheard lyrics, I used to think Abba were asking, 'how does it feel that you won the war?' in the chorus of their *Waterloo* retrospective. A suitable question surely. Turns out it was actually a statement about being defeated in the war. And I still have very little idea what Manfred Mann are singing about on Bruce Springsteen's *Blinded by the Light*. Though I dearly love the song and have discovered it was featured (yay!) on *Disco Rocket.*

### Cut!

The snag with these compilations was that several tracks were edited or faded out early in order to fit up to twelve of them on each side. I'm assured on the great-global-webternet that one side of a vinyl album could hold between twenty-two and forty minutes of material depending on the sound quality. Clearly the makers were making those little grooves very snug indeed to include as many tracks as possible. Barry

Biggs' number three chart hit *Side Show*, was featured on the 1977 collection *Hit Action*, but I still feel a pang of frustration about the way they cut the second verse to fit it onto the album. The whole second verse! It only had two verses. Couldn't they just have dropped the instrumental break and then faded the last chorus? I mean that's a whole interesting bit, with words and everything. Gone! Sighs heavily.

**Top Five ELO Favourites**
*Wild West Hero*
*Living Thing*
*Rockaria!*
*Last Train to London*
*Confusion*

**10-4**
In this period I was recording the likes of *Dat* by Pluto Shervington, *Harmour Love* by Syreeta (at that time I think she was married to Stevie Wonder), Hank Mizell's *Jungle Rock*, *Stay* by Jackson Browne and The Bay City Rollers' version of *I Only Wanna Be With You*. These songs may mean very little to you, having been swallowed by history and the hundreds of other feelgood songs, but they were gold dust to me. Happy upbeat numbers, that made me smile and jig a bit, and capturing a few minutes of them on tape was my Shangri=La.

There was also that CB radio classic *Convoy* by CW McCall, closely followed by *Convoy GB*. I was at that all-boys grammar school when *Convoy* came out, it was

1976 and I was in the second form. (The school numbering system was confusing back then, if you were in the second year, they called it the second form, thank goodness it's now year seven or nine or fourteen or fifty-three. Much more straightforward. 😊)

Liquorice legs (black and yellow stripy socks) and bags (trousers with huge side pockets and twelve-button waistbands) were all the rage. And we were fascinated by the language of *Convoy*, '10-4, breaker one-nine, bear in the air, Rubber Duck, Pig Pen.' (I have to confess I always thought Pig Pen was Big Ben till I just looked it up.) Then Laurie Lingo and the Dipsticks came along with their Super Scouse and Plastic Chicken on the M1 motorway. Not quite as butch or glamorous but it made us laugh all the same.

### Crackle and Hiss

At some point I inherited an old valve radio from my uncle, and I spent many happy if sometimes tense hours in my room, with a microphone blue-tacked to this old red and cream radio trying to capture my latest favourite. It had a bad habit of suddenly crackling loudly smack in the middle of a song, thus ruining in my mind the whole recording. The other danger was someone knocking at the door or walking in just as CW McCall was hitting his stride and about to put the hammer down. What joy of joys when my parents bought themselves a cassette radio which meant I could record direct without picking up any background noises off or cries of 'David your tea's ready.' Heaven.

But that came later. Who knows how many hours I whiled away before that, my finger hovering over the record button, waiting to capture *Golden Years* or *Don't Go Breaking My Heart* or *Red Light Spells Danger*. And just for your info, the valve radio sat beside my cassette recorder on the very same desk that I am now sitting at typing this book.

### And Up Ten Places

My favourite show was the Sunday night top twenty on 247 Radio One. (Inflation has pushed that up to the top forty now of course). Back then Tom Browne, then Simon Bates, then Tony Blackburn played the top twenty from six till seven on a Sunday night. It was the undisputed high point of my weekend, immediately followed by the absolute low point, as the only thing left after that was school the next day.

I began recording that hour in its entirety and in May 1976 I went one step further. I wrote it down! So began several years of notebooks jammed with the top twenty listings. My spelling of the names of some of the titles and artists was interesting. Sadly I no longer have the notebooks, or I'd give you a few entertaining examples. In my defence bands do have unusual names. I mean Splodgenessabounds – how do you spell that? It's all right now, I've got the great-global-webternet for checking it, back then it wasn't in my Redruth English Dictionary.

This became less of a problem when I started buying *Record Mirror* every Saturday, this weekly music paper printed the Radio One top forty, so it was easy to just cut it out and stick it in. But something was lost in translation. Writing stuff down always makes you feel more invested in the information. I often take a notebook to church these days. Partly to scribble something I hear and partly to doodle my own meandering thoughts.

I did pore over those printed chart listings though and in some ways strolling to the paper shop to pick up my ordered copy of *Record Mirror* became a weekend highlight. Bit of a downer as I did that on Saturday mornings, so the rest of the weekend could only be a disappointment. Whilst in Cornwall I did at some point discover that Radio Luxembourg also broadcast chart numbers late at night. But the reception was poor and I didn't stick with it. Radio Luxembourg's history meant nothing to me then, I had been too young for the Pirate age.

### Flipping

My sister used to babysit for a couple who lived opposite us in Alexandra Close. Well, she didn't babysit the couple, she was there for the baby. I have vivid memories of waiting until the couple had gone out in their black Ford capri, and then zipping over there to munch on their excellent cheese and tomato sandwiches, on white bread of course. Then my sister and I would watch various things, including the spooky *Tales of the Unexpected*. Very exciting. Maybe *Hammer House of Horror* too.

Not only that, but the couple had a K-Tel Record Selector. Yes! Absolutely! One of those flip-forward holders, full of albums that we didn't have in our house. The selector had a new space age design (I can assure you of that because I've just watched the old advert on YouTube), and you simply pulled the first album forward and one by one the others flicked after it until you spotted the one you were looking for and could deftly remove it. There were most likely a few K-Tel compilations in there. I seem to remember *20 Dynamic Hits*, featuring Sly and the Family Stone singing *Family Affair* and The Fortunes with *Storm in a Tea Cup*.

But the album that sticks in my mind is Wings' *Band on the Run*. I recall studying the famous folk on the cover, black-suited and wide-eyed and looking guilty in the prison spotlight. I probably didn't know many of the faces, but that didn't stop it being a wonderfully obscure and fascinating picture.

The couple across the way also had two Afghan hounds which I was paid to brush for a short time. I'm amazed I did that now as I'm not at ease around dogs, and the laddie dog was no small fry. I think his lady friend was called Sheba, but I can't recall his name. I can still hear the sound of the brush scraping through the long hair though. And as worried as I was, I didn't get eaten. Phew. But we're not here to discuss Afghan hounds, back to the music.

### Museum Pieces

From time to time I watch clips of pop stars from the early '70s on YouTube. They fascinate me, the way they were products of their time. How they sang, what they wore, how they danced, and the haircuts they had. How they came across as people and performers. I'm talking about the likes of The Three Degrees (*When Will I See You Again*), Mac and Katie Kissoon (*Sugar Candy Kisses*), Guys and Dolls (*There's a Whole Lot of Loving*), R and J Stone (*We Do It*) and Pickettywitch (*That Same Old Feeling*). Songs which seem mostly cheesy now, but that's almost the wonder of it. We wouldn't conjure up hits like these nowadays. I'm so glad someone took the time to load these old clips online.

These songs were the soundtrack of my early years in Cornwall. And these performances seem like living museum pieces to me, bringing back a distant feeling, and the odd hazy memory from another time and another culture. Whenever I watch I'm back there again in some half-remembered, out-of-focus way. It's like getting in a time machine, transporting me back to an era that barely seems real now, and yet something deep inside resonates. Music can do that, can't it.

These songs bring up something in me, remind me a little of who I was, open a window on the past. They're like pop artefacts, rescued from a foreign land, from a distant point on the musical horizon, now fading into history.

### Five Songs You May Have Forgotten About
*Couldn't Get It Right* (Climax Blues Band)
*Glass of Champagne* (Sailor)
*Walking Down Madison* (Kirsty McColl)
*Tulane* (Steve Gibbons Band)
*It Takes Two to Tango* (Richard Myhill)

I was going to include the single *Requiem* by Slik, but... well you know what it's like when you revisit something and it just wasn't quite as outstanding as you remember...

Some space for any thoughts, doodlings, scribblings, top fives, or musical memories of your own.

**Side Two Track One**

One memorable school music lesson (probably in 1977) we were invited to bring in our favourite track. I didn't. I'd be keeping my head down on a week like that. I realise now I am shy and private, two things which don't always go hand in hand. But as mentioned earlier, I was often cautious to tell the truth about the music I really liked. Still am sometimes. Catchy and cool don't always rub shoulders. I've frequently wondered about this, why popular records are dismissed as commercial. And why music which is harder to listen to is deemed to be superior. So with that in mind, I joined in at school with the music that was acceptable but kept schtum about other songs. That was the wonderful thing about liking punk later on. It was cool and laddie, and also really meant something to me.

But back to *that* music lesson... I remember well the record that one of the lads brought in. David Bowie's sixth studio album *Aladdin Sane*. So called because when Bowie recorded it the madness of fame was getting to him a bit, and so *A Lad Insane* made reference to that. Side two kicks off with a little track called *Time*. And that was the requested song.

As our music teacher put the needle to the groove we waited in nervous, gleeful anticipation, because Bowie was about to sing naughty words. No need to repeat them here. It was just a typical schoolboy ruse. Let's see if we can get Sir to play a rude song in class. Well, he did and I'm sure we chortled cheekily behind our hands. But a little bit of me was horrified too, and the experience got seared into my memory. No doubt Sir had heard it all before, he may even have had the album for all I know. But the image being sung about was stark and raw, and I had conflicted feelings, it felt a little invasive to me as the listener. Too raw, too revealing.

I still have mixed feelings about swearing in songs, though I'd soon be hearing a hefty smattering of huffing, frapping and blumming. The punks didn't mince their words, they were protesting about mediocrity and conformity, and they came with a verbal dropkick. But I keep digressing, back to Mr Bowie. I only ever bought a couple of his studio albums, *Lodger* (released in 1979) because I loved *Sound and Vision*, and *Scary Monsters (and Super Creeps)* (1980) because of *Ashes to Ashes*. I like a lot of Bowie's songs these days, but those two are still my favourites.

In 1992 he performed at The Freddie Mercury Tribute Concert for AIDS Awareness, and after singing *Heroes*, he knelt on the stage and prayed the Lord's Prayer over the microphone. There were seventy-two thousand people there, and the concert was beamed into seventy-six countries around the world, with an audience of perhaps a billion. Not only that, you can still find the clip on YouTube now, so who knows how many others continue to find it and listen to those timeless words given to us by Jesus. A prayer we can all pray. Wherever we are, and whoever is or isn't watching.

**Five David Bowie Favourites**
*Young Americans*
*Changes*
*Life on Mars*

40

*Golden Years*
*Sound and Vision*

## £2.50

Some time in '76 or '77 I bought *Abba's Greatest Hits* in Appledore. We went there for the day to see my aunt and uncle, and I purchased the cassette for, I believe, £2.50. I had already acquired The Drifters' *24 Original Hits* and The Beach Boys' *20 Golden Greats*. So these three formed the first building blocks in my record collection. I got them on cassette as it meant I could play them in my room on my tape machine.

By September 1977 I had added two Queen albums. *A Night at the Opera* and *A Day at the Races*. Both named after Marx Brothers movies I believe. I had been a Queen fan ever since first hearing the irresistibly catchy *Killer Queen*, a number two hit in 1974, and no doubt *Bohemian Rhapsody* and *You're My Best Friend* both sealed the deal. When *Somebody to Love* was released in 1977 I was besotted and decided I loved it more than the classic *Rhapsody*. So you can imagine my heartbreak when it only made number two after crashing into the charts at number four, the highest new entry since records began. Well, since records began in my notebook. We heard the news in our school lunch break, sitting at the back of our classroom, our ears pressed close to the tiny transistor.

Perhaps there was some lesson in that for me about not always being able to get what you want. I think The Rolling Stones sang about that. Time and again the charts let me down and refused to turn my favourite

41

numbers into chart-topping hits. Life was so unfair. After Freddy Mercury died in 1991 George Michael and Queen took a live version of the song to number one, so I felt that was a worthy result.

But I also have another recollection about Freddy Mercury. Between first hearing he was ill in 1991, and then hearing of his sad death, I never said a prayer for him at all. And it was a sobering thought. I was happy to hook into the news stories around the situation but never thought to send up a prayer for the man who had brought me so much musical joy. Those two Queen cassettes were the first studio albums I ever owned. The first two collections that were not 'best of' compilations. And I played them a lot. A lot a lot a lot.

I did send up prayers for Bob Marley when I heard he was ill. I had loved his laid-back Jamaican sound, that lilt made you feel as if the sun was shining. I was especially grabbed by *Jammin'* and later *Three Little Birds*, but I loved his other songs too, and I later found that the punks did as well. Stiff Little Fingers covered his *Johnny Was*, and The Clash did another reggae classic, Junior Murvin's *Police and Thieves*, as well as writing their own *White Man in Hammersmith Palais* and *Bankrobber*. Reggae and punk had protest and outcry in common.

### Top ~~Five~~ Six Reggae Favourites
*Dat* (Pluto Shervington)
*Three Little Birds* (Bob Marley and the Wailers)
*Jammin'* (Bob Marley and the Wailers)
*Message in a Bottle* (The Police)
*Red Red Wine* (UB40)

*I Can See Clearly Now* (Johnny Nash)

When our youngest daughter Lucy was very little, I snuck into a greenhouse in the rain and had a great time jigging with her in my arms while singing a rough version of that last song to her.

**Four Singles**

In the summer of 1977, not long before we moved from Cornwall to Weston-super-Mare, I went to town and bought four vinyl singles. Possibly from Woolworths, I can't be sure. *It's Your Life, I Knew the Bride, We're All Alone,* and *The Crunch* or perhaps (dare I say it) it might have been *You Got What It Takes* by Showaddywaddy.

Those doowop guys in the crepes and drapes were the boy band for my generation. They've long since fallen out of favour, yet we loved 'em. And *Under the Moon of Love* was number one for three weeks! Plus they had four number two singles. So we weren't the only fans.

I was fourteen and we had just acquired a hefty hi-fi system with stereo speakers, up until that point we had only had the aforementioned Dansette mono record player, housed in that blue box strong enough for a boy to sit on. Those classics by Smokie, Dave Edmunds, Rita Coolidge and The Rah Band (or maybe Showaddywaddy) began a busy four years of record collecting which ended around Christmas '81 when I was given Abba's album *The Visitors* – their last studio album for forty years.

What is noticeable here in '77 is a complete lack of punk purchases, even though it was punk's year zero and the snarling and spitting was well under way. That lot would have to wait.

### Top Five Abba Favourites
*Take a Chance on Me*
*When I Kissed the Teacher* (from *Arrival*)
*That's Me* (from *Arrival*)
*The Winner Takes It All*
*Dance (While the Music Still Goes On)*

### Jumpers and Flares
I never had a safety pin through my nose. Or my cheek. Or lip. Or chin. Or anywhere else. And when we first began to hear the savage strains of the Sex Pistols, the news terrified me. At the time Showaddywaddy had gone to number one with *Under the Moon of Love* and as mentioned, that was much more my thing. (When I typed them in just then it came out as Showaffywaggy which would be a good name for an indie group.)

I was still plugged into the ever-so-slightly cheesy, middle-of-the-road chart songs. Leo Sayer was feeling like dancing, and Elkie Brooks was telling us about Pearl being a singer, Demis Roussos was bringing us *Forever and Ever*, and Johnny Mathis was heading for the Christmas number one. The charts were fun and easy on the ears. Everyone wore smiles and jumpers and flares. Why did we need these sneering, spitting danger men?

There's a great moment in one of my favourite documentaries when a smartly suited Important Person looks at the camera and claims that punk poses a greater threat than Russian communism. Help! The world was lurching towards complete Johnny Rottenness, and nothing was safe anymore. Funny to think that it wouldn't be long before the songs from these punk misfits would become the love of my life, and end up as tunes that I still play to this day. More on that later.

The Pistols' first single *Anarchy in the UK* was released in the Autumn of 1976, it went into the charts at thirty-eight and stuck there for three weeks. Then it disappeared. Phew! I wasn't even aware of it at the time, but the trouble was clearly over. Anarchy was done and dusted. 1977 came around and David Soul (of *Starsky and Hutch* fame) nabbed the top spot for four weeks with the biggest selling single of the year. All was well. The jumpers and flares were still in.

### Jubilee

Not for long though, as the Queen and country got all decked out to celebrate twenty-five years of the top job, Johnny and his pals made a bit of a brouhaha as they put out their second single, a jubilee song of a different kind. There is still debate today about whether they secretly knocked Rod Stewart off the top spot, but according to the official records, in early June 1977 *God Save the Queen* made number two in the charts.

The likely layabouts would soon be on Top of the Pops too with their follow up *Pretty Vacant*. The floodgates were open and all manner of three-minute singles were on the way. The revolution had arrived. Though there was no sign of it when Radio One celebrated ten years of pop-picking fun, dear listeners.

### Fire

In 1977 Radio One turned ten. Yay! Double figures. They celebrated by bringing out the helpfully titled double album *Ten Years of Hits on Radio One*. That record introduced me to a hefty number of '60s classics. *Whiter Shade of Pale, Something in the Air, The Mighty Quinn, Fire, Flowers in the Rain* (the first song ever played on Radio One), *I Heard it Through the Grapevine, Love Grows Where My Rosemary Goes.* That last one was actually a 1970s hit and the song that was number one the day my wife was born. *Return to Sender* was at the top when I was born, five years before Tony Blackburn and his pals started broadcasting on the Beeb.

My sister and I clubbed together and bought the *Ten Years of Hits* album, with that huge red 1 emblazoned across the cover, and I'm happy to say, I don't think any of the tracks had been macheted down or faded early. It didn't however contain any tracks by The Beatles, The Who, The Kinks or The Stones. I later discovered The Beatles have been very protective of their music so maybe the other bands were too. Or maybe just too expensive. Or perhaps they were down the shop when the call came.

Queen's *Bohemian Rhapsody* was also noticeable by its absence. What?! Hadn't it been voted the best song ever in some important poll somewhere? And wasn't it one of the most successful number ones? And yet here it was, not there. I was a little bit put out. I still played the album loads though. By now we had moved to Weston-super-Mare with our new stereo hi-fi system, so we got this on vinyl and pumped it out over the snazzy speakers.

And just reflecting on the early sound of The Who, when I hear *My Generation* I can't help thinking they were the forerunners of punk, with their abrasive attitude and aggressive stage presence. Their lyrics weren't exactly gentle either, their startling line about dying before being old has gone down in musical history. Like the Sex Pistols they missed the top spot due to a safer, calmer option – The Seekers beat them to it with *The Carnival is Over*.

The cover of their first album, also called *My Generation*, featured an overhead shot of the band looking up, and it's one that was emulated by The Specials on their first album. I'm sure I've seen a similar photo of The Clash too but now can't find it. Seven of the twelve tracks on that first Who album were under three minutes and the whole album was only thirty-five minutes long.

### OCD

One odd and long-lasting behavioural problem kicked in around that time, strangely linked to a Bee Gees song. For decades I have struggled with OCD, and I clearly recall getting into a habit back in 1978, as I said 'night to my folks each evening, of needing to silently add the word 'fever', in my head. Odd I know but these things often have strange and unexpected roots. If I silently added this line from the song a couple of times I felt somehow safer. Not sure how long that phase lasted, and I hasten to add I don't in any way blame the Bee Gees for it.

I can trace my struggle with obsessive behaviour back much further in fact, to an event when I was a lot younger and we lived in Stoke-on-Trent. (The Bee Gees weren't involved.) I must have been somewhere around five or six when, attending a birthday party, I discovered to my horror that, wrapped in the folds of the present I gave to my friend, there was the broken plastic stem of a toy pipe. I loved those tiny yellow and brown pipes (my granddad smoked a pipe) and I had bought one but broken it and then lost track of the bits. I felt deeply embarrassed and foolish to see this piece of pipe emerge when the present was unwrapped. I had been exposed as a bit of a failure. I felt I should have checked it, sorted it, made sure somehow that this would not happen in public like this. I was and am easily embarrassed and that set a marker in my life. Checking obsessively remains a problem for me to this day.

Around the time of the *Night Fever* habit I also made the gaff of posting a draft of a church magazine article in the red post box rather than through the vicarage letterbox. In my defence a) the post box was right outside the vicarage gate, and b) I am an airhead and easily get distracted. But again I was embarrassed and felt a failure at having made this gaff, and this only added to the pressure I felt to check and double check and triple check things. Therapy session over. 😊

**Five Bee Gee Songs Covered by The Dee Gees (aka The Foo Fighters)**
*Night Fever*
*More Than a Woman*
*Tragedy*
*You Should Be Dancing*
*Shadow Dancing* (originally recorded by Andy Gibb)

Some space for any thoughts, doodlings, scribblings, top fives, or musical memories of your own.

**Grease is the Word**

In the summer of 1978 our church youth group went to Yeovil for a week, to help out with a kids club there. We slept in a church hall, and in between the activities we wandered around town scaring the seagulls as a rowdy bunch. Albeit a rowdy *Christian* bunch. 10cc were at number one in the charts with their song *Dreadlock Holiday*, and so we could often be heard wailing in the streets about reggae and cricket and Jamaica as we walked along. The songs from *Grease* were also around, and the epic *Jilted John* too. So we made a right old racket about these things as we filled the streets with our hearty screeching.

I wince now when I think about it, but at the time it was a blast. I was fifteen and optimistic and surrounded by friends, so why wouldn't you sing about being in love with a girl called Julie and getting your heart broken when she dumped you for Gordon. Why not caterwaul about those summer days as they drift away, and – ahh – these summer nights. Perhaps these things prepared me in some way for the many times years later when I would go into the streets doing Christian drama and mime.

When I read this back now it sounds funny, unintentionally funny. The notion that wailing *Jilted John* could somehow prepare me for communicating about God and life and hope. And yet maybe it's all connected. Something of that experience gave me courage and stamina for the later adventures. One experience feeding another experience. (Or maybe it was all just a sign, a foreshadowing, signalling the fact that I was the kind of person willing to look foolish in public.)

But what's to say that being willing to sing about not liking cricket... but loving it, in the street didn't prep me in some way for being willing to mime about the crucifixion. To stand there with my arms outstretched knowing that this was the most important thing in the world. This thing I was portraying about God and Jesus and life and death and sacrifice and surprise. We never know what God might use to shape us. I don't think for a second that God only uses what we deem to be spiritual and important to prepare us for future things.

### Top ~~Five~~ Ten Queen Favourites

*I Can't Live With You* (from *Innuendo*)
*Killer Queen*
*Good Old-Fashioned Lover Boy*
*Don't Stop Me Now*
*Somebody to Love*
*You're My Best Friend*
*Spread Your Wings*
*Death On Two Legs* (from *A Night at the Opera*)
*Play the Game*
*Hammer to Fall*

### One Gallon or Two

There was once a time, back in the days of yore, when garage attendants used to come out and put petrol in your tank for you. I know that for sure because I was once one such attendant. In the summer of '78 I took a job working four hours every Saturday at a nearby garage. I got 50p an hour ('50p? You were lucky! We used to dream of getting 50p!').

I'd start at 5pm and knock off at 9pm, then jump on my bike and pedal for home, veering off for the chippie on my way. Then I'd be back in time to watch the latest episode of *The Professionals*. It was a great experience for learning about the world of work, (the garage that is, not *The Professionals*. Bodie and Doyle were employed in a whole other kind of *profession*.) But serving petrol taught me a good deal about relating to customers, cashing up, dealing with credit cards. All that sort of thing.

Back then we had those sliding credit card imprinters, where you placed the card under a couple of bits of paper and hoped like mad it wouldn't get rucked up as you pushed the slider across. The mechanism always seemed stiff and needing plenty of white-knuckle shoving. We could only dream of the days of chip and pin, and tap and go. Apparently some businesses still keep these machines for emergencies, in case the power goes down.

I've been racking my brains for any musical memories from that time, but I keep coming up short. I was offered the job when a friend gave it up because of doing his school exams, and I do have a vague recollection of hanging around down there with a couple of church youth group mates when our friend was still working there in late '78. The Cars were the new big thing at the time. (Did you see what I did there – garage – cars?)

Anyway, seven years before The Cars became widely known for the use of their song *Drive* with those powerful images at Live Aid, they released *My Best Friend's Girl*. It came out as a picture disc, but I think the version I bought was simply imprinted on red vinyl. I've just looked it up and seen it for the first time, a suitably swish red car on a white background. Picture discs and coloured discs were becoming more prevalent as collectors' items, plus it was another way to sell a few more records.

I was the proud possessor of ELO's *Sweet Talking Woman* on purple vinyl. Can still see it now in my mind's eye. In 1979 Alan Price bought out a double A-sided single on a red heart-shaped disc, possibly for Valentine's Day, *Baby of Mine* and *Just for You*. There was talk at one time of records being in some way hyped. Paying Janice and Joe Bloggs to pop down to their local store and buy a job lot of one disc. Certain record stores provided sales figures for the charts, so the easiest way to get to number one was by hiking up the numbers at these shops.

### Tuned

I've just been reminded once again of my ignorance about pop music. Bono is the lead singer of U2, and in his autobiography, *Surrender,* he describes The Rolling Stones 1978 song *Miss You* as disco. And I realise now I'd come across that description before. But back when I loved it I had no idea. Didn't sound like disco to me, just sounded like a great tune which I could play over and over. It was a world-wide 'smash' as they used to say, and no wonder. Disco was big back then. I knew that *Boogie Wonderland* and *Disco Inferno* and *Disco Duck* were disco songs, not least because it kind of says so on the tin (or the label). But The Stones? Wow. Who knew? Well, Bono for a start.

I realise again that I hear but I don't hear, I'm tuned but I'm not tuned. I'm conditioned. I guess it's like anything, we often see and hear what we want to, what we're used to, what we know. What we think we're looking for. I've just read an article about a guy who watched the film *Groundhog Day* every day for a year, in the pandemic lockdown. He went through various phases, but saw things he'd never seen before, and the film brought new experiences to him.

Makes me want to do something similar, to reach a point where I'm not trying to control what I see and hear, but learn something new from it. Yesterday, following a conversation with a friend about seeing but not seeing, I wrote this.

### ? ? ? ? ?
Are we moving too fast?
Has life settled into such a pace that
We are no longer able to appreciate the view?
To see to hear to smell to taste to touch,
Is there still a time for everything?
A time to slow down, a time to pause,
A time to gaze into the soft unknown,
And appreciate the beauty in a single blade of grass.
Do we feel too urgently pressured,
To stop and ease a stick into the spokes of life?

Can we still surprise ourselves with the gift
Of a calming breath,
While the winds of progress tug at our sleeves?

### New Music

Sometime in early '79 I decided I needed some new music in my life. I needed a new favourite band. Never mind about school exams and any possible future career. I needed to sort out a new favourite group! I'd been very lax in keeping up with Queen, I had still only ever bought those two albums on cassette. So apart from a couple of singles, (*We Are the Champions* and *Spread Your Wings*) the relationship was kind of lukewarm. 'He never phones he never calls...' etc.

I chatted to my mates at school about it, one of whom was a massive Dr Feelgood fan. I'd never heard of them till meeting Simon. For a while I considered Thin Lizzy. They were rocky and cool and publicly acceptable. I liked *The Boys Are Back in Town*, and had bought their single *Waiting For an Alibi*. But the relationship never took off. And anyway, I was in a drama class with Stefan and Mel. Stef was my best mate and he was secretly in love with Mel. And Mel was a punk. Big into The Clash.

Before I knew it Stef had put his Supertramp album aside and was playing *Another Music in a Different Kitchen* by Buzzcocks. And more importantly, *Give 'Em Enough Rope* by The Clash. Could it be possible? Could I swap the likes of Status Quo, the Bee Gees and Electric Light Orchestra (from here on referred to as ELO) for Joe Strummer and his gang?

Well... yes and no. I never stopped listening to the other stuff, but I did embrace that raucous rabble. Full on. My life took a seismic shift. All that stuff I had hated and feared in 1976 suddenly became my home. The songs were fast and furious and surprisingly melodic. Under the sneering and the gunfire delivery there were good tunes.

### Docs

I have a couple of favourite music documentaries. The first, *Punk Britannia*, tells of the rise of pub rock ('70-'76, Dr Feelgood were part of this), punk ('76-'78), and post punk ('78 and beyond). I love the narrative style, it's full of rock'n'roll eloquence, in my 'umble 'pinion. I knew nothing of pub rock until I saw this in 2012. It was 35 years since the fateful 'year of punk' in 1977 and the Beeb decided to celebrate with a three-part analysis of this riotous, ragged ruckus.

Pub rock began in 1970 when an American trio knocked on the door of a London pub and asked if they could play there. After that pubs became the venues for bands who couldn't get a stage elsewhere. In the documentary these blaze-trailing rockers are described as the gateway generation for punk. The bands had superb names – Eggs Over Easy, Bees Make Honey, Ducks Deluxe, The Kursaal Flyers, Kilburn and the High Roads, and the great Dr Feelgood. These guys paved the way for the revolution to come with their frenetic take on rock'n'roll and blues. The London pubs benefited too. No longer just musty venues for old guys to gossip about footie, they were now full of audiences who'd

57

come to drink and dance. Pub rock laid the foundation for the uprising to come, and some of the bands went on to have success in the New Wave era. Eddie and the Hot Rods, The Kursaal Flyers, and Dr Feelgood all went on to have hit singles. While the Kilburn lads morphed into Ian Durie and the Blockheads, and a few of the Ducks Deluxe guys turned into The Motors, with their classic *Airport*.

My other favourite documentary is another three-parter, *Music for Misfits*, which tells the story of indie music. A genre which began around the same time as punk and has its roots in that make-it-yourself period. The documentary tells an epic, winding tale which includes the likes of Stock Aitken and Waterman, the KLF, and the battle of Britpop. (More on Britpop later.)

### Four Hundred Years

I'll watch most music documentaries, even those about artists and bands I never listen to, I'm fascinated by the stories of how they get together, create their material and perform together. And sometimes break up. I love seeing where folks get their ideas and what they do with them. And I love beginnings, seeing how new things start up.

I'm currently reading Nick Hornby's book about the musician Prince and the author Charles Dickens. It's called unsurprisingly *Dickens and Prince*. I only know three or four songs by Prince, and have barely read any Dickens. I've dipped into *A Christmas Carol* and was supposed to read *A Tale of Two Cities* for my English Literature O' level. I kept putting off opening the hefty tome and convinced myself I could read it the night before my exam. I know, in a single night!! #Naiveorwhat…

Needless to say I didn't manage it and have still not read it, though I know it opens with the great line about the best of times and the worst of times, and ends with the line about doing a far better thing than I've ever done. But I love Hornby's book, because it's full of inspiring stuff about two great creatives. Did you know that Dickens wrote four million words? This book is roughly somewhere in the region of forty thousand. So you get the picture. And Prince left us so many unreleased songs, they could go on releasing new albums by him for the next three or four hundred years. Three or four hundred years!!! And enough new songs for that little Corvette, and that rain, and the beret to end up being all the colours of the rainbow. Not just red, purple, and raspberry.

**Free Trade**

Along with The Clash, Mel in our drama class introduced us to The Jam, Blondie, Stiff Little Fingers and Buzzcocks. I was aware of Blondie because they'd had an infectious hit with *Denis*. And we didn't really need much introduction to the Sex Pistols. They were notorious. The Jam, The Clash and Stiff Little Fingers (their first album *Inflammable Material* is still just about the rawest collection I've ever heard) became my favourite bands of the time.

Buzzcocks meanwhile gave the world three crucial things (in my 'umble 'pinion) – they invited the Sex

Pistols to play a hugely influential gig in the Lesser Free Trade Hall in Manchester in June '76, before Mr Rotten and his chums were famous/infamous. Only about forty folk turned up and saw them, but they were the kind of folk who went on to do stuff. Morrissey of The Smiths was there, so too Ian Curtis, Bernard Sumner and Peter Hook, who then formed Joy Division and later went on to become New Order, plus Tony Wilson who founded Factory Records and the Hacienda club. Journalist Paul Morley who went on to write for the NME was there, and Mark E. Smith who then founded the band The Fall. Other bands and musicians who weren't there were later influenced by those who were. The likes of Green Day, Nirvana, Blur.

Buzzcocks also gave us the classic punk-pop single *Ever Fallen in Love (With Someone You Shouldn't've)* and before that, they inadvertently kicked off an entire musical genre. Indie music. In October 1976 the young Buzzcock lads wanted to find out what they sounded like so they discovered they could record and produce 1000 of their own singles for £500, something unheard of back then. To release a record you had to be with a proper company, but no. Here come these upstarts from Manchester recording their own four songs! They entitled the EP *Spiral Scratch* and that was just the start.

Before long Joy Division took inspiration and did the same. Buzzcocks had begun a revolution in the music industry. Independent labels like Factory and Rough Trade started up and the rest is history. A whole swathe of music has followed in its wake and Indie lives on to this day.

**Top Five Blondie Favourites**
*Sunday Girl*
*Heart of Glass*
*Slow Motion* (from *Eat to the Beat*)
*Picture This*
*Dreaming*

## Three Chords

Punk inspired all kinds of people to have a go. Many did not end up in successful bands, but they went into comedy and journalism and other unexpected futures. Charlie Higson and Paul Whitehouse formed a punk band, but later discovered they could make people laugh for a living and went on to fame with *The Fast Show*.

A good number of singers and musicians who would later emerge in synth and New Romantic bands were inspired to start playing. And even Pulp's Jarvis Cocker, who wouldn't be truly famous till the Britpop '90s, cites the new thinking and outlook of punk as part of his inspiration. He saw the future when he read some instructions in a punk fanzine which said something like: 'Here's a chord, here's another, here's a third, now form a band.' He was one of many who felt it might just be worth giving it a try.

Comedians, fashion designers, artists, writers, journalists and who-knows-who-else were all inspired by punk to have a go. Watch any punk documentary and sooner or later someone will say something like, 'I didn't think I was good enough, but then I saw the Pistols and thought, well if they can do it...' Punk's ethos was don't wait for permission, or training, or funding, or equipment. Have a go. It was a creative explosion. They were years ahead of Nike with their slogan *Just Do It*.

Nowadays the great-global-webternet has made that more possible than ever. I can write this book because I can publish it free. I don't need a publishing company or a think-tank or advertisers or much of a budget. Punk lives on.

A few years back I wrote a short book called *Dead Prophets Society*, drawing on the Old Testament writings of Ezekiel. It was about a group of punks challenging the system in a dying town. I love the way Ezekiel is unafraid to do so much weird stuff in order to wake people up – building models, punching holes in his wall, cooking on cow dung, shaving his head – and it seemed to me that he and the other prophets had a kind of punk spirit about them. Refusing to accept the system and doing what they could to make folk think again.

So I told this fictional tale, and wove some of Ezekiel's activities into it, I'm not sure it worked but it was worth trying. You have to try. Even just trying to write a tale that merged punk and prophecy was perhaps in itself punky and prophetic. The prophets worried people and made them sit up and take notice. Writing a book about pop music and God, now that's got to be worth trying surely.

### Bay City Ramones

And now for an unexpected question. Did you know The Ramones were inspired by The Bay City Rollers? Yes indeed they were. How's that for a culture clash, Scottish boy band and American punk. The BCR boys had a massive hit with *Bye Bye Baby*, six weeks at number one in 1975. When they tried to break America though they were told in no uncertain terms they couldn't possibly release that. It was a Four Seasons classic. They wrote it and already had a hit with it.

So the tartan-trousered chaps rolled up with *Saturday Night*, which began with an audience-involving chant, using the letters from the word Saturday. The Ramones spotted this and thought, we need a chant like that. The result was all that hey-ho-ing at the get-go of the *Blitzkrieg Bop*.

The Four Seasons gave plenty of other folks big hits. *Working My Way Back to You* was a number one for The Detroit Spinners, *Can't Take My Eyes Off You*, was a top five hit for Andy Williams, *Silence is Golden* was a number one for The Tremeloes, *Let's Hang On* went to number eleven for Darts, and *The Sun Ain't Gonna Shine Any More* was a number one for The Walker Brothers. All first recorded by Frankie Valli and The Four Seasons. And there are others, but you get the picture.

### Exons

Meanwhile, back in the late '70s, I was discovering other bands and singers, Nick Lowe, Wreckless Eric, Magazine, The Undertones, The Ramones, The Vapors, Eddie and the Hot Rods, X-Ray Specs, Generation X, The Boomtown Rats, Elvis Costello and the Attractions, and Ian Dury and the Blockheads. It was just a fantastic time full of new music and guitar bands. As punk subsided and gave way to New Wave, bands like The Jags, The Members, The Police, The Only Ones, Adam and the Ants, XTC, The Pretenders and others came through.

There were a fair number of one hit wonders, and I got many of them. I never went to any gigs, I was too much of a quiet country boy, but I hunted down the music. I ordered back copies of all of The Jam's and The Clash's singles. Both bands were big on bringing out stand-alone singles between their albums. I wanted the lot.

Exons Records was the go-to place, opposite the bank I worked in. And I'll always remember the day I walked in and saw, right there in the rack, quietly waiting for me, no fuss or bother, no sneering or spitting... the third album by The Clash. *London Calling*. It had come out that day. The future had landed. I scooped it up, bought it for a fiver and hugged it all the way home on the bus.

When I'd first got into The Clash it was via their second album, and I'd been in the dying days of my final school year. Now my favourite punks had brought out this double album, packed with nineteen tracks to shake up the world once more. I must have raced up to my room when I got in, put it on the turntable and soaked up the songs.

### New Arrivals

Joe, Paul, Mick and Topper had been at a low ebb after *Give 'Em Enough Rope*. There'd been the follow up four-track EP *The Cost Of Living* which included the bombastic *I Fought the Law*. But what then? Punk was fading fast and the explosive originality of that three-chord outcry was on the wane. The Pistols had long since imploded. So what to do now? They steeled themselves, went into a secluded studio for six months, hung out as friends, and worked hard rehearsing, writing and recording together. *London Calling* was born in that intense half-year.

These are the kind of stories I love, when an artist or a group are down and out, and from the dust and the rubble something magnificent and original emerges. That double LP came out in December 1979. Twenty-one years later my wife gave me the album on CD as a present, and when I put it on I couldn't believe how good it still sounded. And how much I still loved it. Another twenty-two years have passed and I still play it.

When I consider my all-time favourite album I'm torn between that one and *Give 'Em Enough Rope*. The critics will tell you *London Calling* is by far the better album, but they didn't play *Give 'Em Enough Rope* over and over and over and over in their bedroom on that old Dansette blue box record player. Or maybe they did. But you just can't beat an experience like that.

I was sixteen and angst-ridden and those ten tracks perfectly hit the spot. *Give 'Em Enough Rope* explodes from the speakers from the get-go with the first track *Safe European Home* and then it just doesn't let up. Apart from one perfectly formed slightly gentler number about friendship. *Stay Free* begins with a line about two friends meeting for the first time at school. And because of that it will always remind me of my old friend Stef.

We both arrived at Broadoak School in the Autumn of 1977, and were put together as the new arrivals. We liked the same music and joked about the same things and fell for the same girl in drama class. Stef was always way cooler than me, but he put up with my awkward bumbling. And then we discovered punk together. And The Clash. And though *Stay Free* goes in a whole other direction, and has nothing else to do with our lives, it doesn't seem to matter.

It does mention being in the pub, and we did do that, at least on one occasion anyway. Underage an' all (I looked about twelve). We skived off cross-country running one afternoon, took a detour and supped something or other in a local establishment. That reminds me of another time when we slipped out of school, (we may have been skiving or it may have been a free lesson) and we wandered with another friend to his house. While we were there Mark put on Blondie's album *Parallel Lines*. That was the day I first heard the sublime and perfectly formed *Sunday Girl*.

I can still see myself sitting on the sofa there, maybe with the sun outside? It feels like it was sunny. But perhaps that was just the music. The only thing I recall clearly from our conversation was Mark saying he liked about half of the tracks and reckoned that was pretty good for an album. I was horrified at the thought of only really liking half the tracks on any LP, but now I think on it I reckon he was mostly right. About a lot of albums anyway.

Though it may tell a different story, *Stay Free* will always take me back to our friendship. And those school days. And the exuberant discovery of *Give 'Em Enough Rope*.

By the time *London Calling* came out I was working in the bank and Stef had moved on to sixth form. Our lives quickly diverged without the glue of school. So as good as *London Calling* is, there's nothing on there that tells me that kind of story.

**Top ~~Five~~ Twelve Clash Favourites**
*White Man in Hammersmith Palais*
*I Fought the Law*
*Tommy Gun*
*Safe European Home* (from *Give 'Em Enough Rope*)
*Julie's Been Working for the Drug Squad* (from *Give 'Em Enough Rope*)
*Rudy Can't Fail* (from *London Calling*)
*Somebody Got Murdered* (from *Sandinista*)
*Should I Stay or Should I Go*
*Hitsville UK* (from *Sandinista*)
*The Card Cheat* (from *London Calling*)
*Gates of the West* (from *The Cost of Living* EP)
*Stay Free* (from *Give 'Em Enough Rope*)

Some space for any thoughts, doodlings, scribblings, top fives, or musical memories of your own.

## Burton Suits

The Jam and The Clash were both inspired by The Sex Pistols. Joe Strummer and Paul Weller both testify to the lane-changing impact of seeing Monsieur Rotten and hearing his motley band play live. But they expressed this new direction very differently. In sound and style. The Clash threw their lot in with the spiky haired, bondage-trousered, ripped t-shirt look. While The Jam pogoed in with thin ties and sharp MOD suits. Something that The Clash couldn't help but comment on in their brilliant, reggae-inspired single *White Man In Hammersmith Palais.* Listen closely and you'll hear mention of suits from the Burton shop, and a line about making money out of rebellion. Mr Strummer didn't name check The Jam of course. But the reference was there. Hidden in plain sight.

## Jammy

The Jam's third album *All Mod Cons*, came out in November 1978. I heard it sometime in early 1979 and it grabbed me by the collar and hoiked me in faster than you could say, 'Paul Weller, Bruce Foxton and Rick Buckler'. There was an energy and an angst that suited me down to the ground. I'd lie on my bed, headphones on, pumping Mr Weller's machine gun vocals into my lugholes. *Setting Sons* came out in 1980, after I'd left school, and for me it set the standard. It featured one single *Eton Rifles*, which propelled the Jam into the top five for the first time. They'd had a bagful of singles and great album tracks before this though, lesser known, but classics as far as I was concerned. Here's a scratch top five from me.

**Top ~~Five~~ Eight Jam Favourites**

*When You're Young*
*Down in the Tube Station*
*Going Underground*
*In the City*
*Away from the Numbers* (from *In the City*)
*'A' Bomb in Wardour Street* (from *All Mod Cons*)
*Beat Surrender*
*Thick as Thieves* (from *Setting Sons*)

**Numbers**

To be honest it's difficult to nail a few favourites, The Jam recorded so many perfectly formed punchy, gutsy tracks. I could go on to list another top ten. But you only have so much time so I'll leave it there. *Away from the Numbers* is a track from their first album, and one I really like because it talks about getting away from the crowds, and grabbing time alone. Perfect for an introvert like me. I want to be useful to people, want to be liked and popular, and believe in trying to help others. But I also find company exhausting at times and have to retreat. I'm encouraged that Jesus needed time out too. The first chapter of Mark's gospel is breathtakingly relentless, and towards the end of it we find Jesus needing to pull back. He grabs time alone in a space devoid of distraction. And he talks to his father. Away from the numbers you might say.

**In the Crowd**

The Jam also recorded *In the Crowd* on *All Mod Cons,* a song about feeling adrift amongst others, anonymous, not knowing who you are, or how to be, losing sight of yourself. Not sure it is exactly about that, probably more about the feeling of being controlled, but as I think on it now it leads me to reflect on my own struggles in a crowd.

I have lived in various communities over the years, so you might think I'd be at home in a group. It's okay when I have a purpose, a thing to do, a job or role to fulfil. Especially if I'm there to lead in some way or share a few thoughts from the front. But just being in a crowd leaves me downbeat and even anxious at times. I can get in a real old twist before going to church on a Sunday. Plus I'm conflicted anyway, as I want to be liked and popular, and part of things, but I also want to be different and unique and to avoid blending in. Something about having cake and eating it. 😊

I'm more relaxed in my own space. And mostly when I'm scribbling an idea or punching keys. That's when I get a sense of doing what I was made to do, being the person I am wired up to be. There's nothing better than sitting in a coffee shop tapping away.


**Life**

Another favourite band at school was Squeeze. We knew all the words to *Cool for Cats*. And *Up the Junction* is just a sublime bit of heartbreaking storytelling. I was working in the bank by the time *Another Nail in My*

*Heart* came out but that was a single I was constantly slipping onto the turntable.

Singers Chris Difford and Glenn Tilbrook wrote all the songs, and I have a quote on my wall from Chris Difford's autobiography *Some Fantastic Place.* He talks about being inspired to write by the things he saw. In other words he drew on life. *Cool for Cats* was inspired by flicking through TV programmes, while *Up The Junction* was inspired by all those *Play For Today* kind of dramas, kitchen sink stuff.

'If you want to be original, tell the truth,' so said CS Lewis. 'What is most personal is most universal,' Henri Nouwen said. And in the movie *The Ghost*, one of the characters explains that the thing which always interests people… is other people. Always people. These few thoughts are among the various sayings I keep in my office to inspire me to draw on everyday life.

Especially when writing about faith. It's so easy to set Christianity in another realm, tempting to separate the kingdom of heaven from gritty reality. But the whole point of God made flesh is that Jesus was totally earthed in normal life. He didn't come from outer space, he didn't beam down fully formed and powerful like The Terminator. He grew slowly inside his mother, minute by minute, second by second, and when the time was right he emerged hungry and tiny and trusting in his new and fragile parents.

'We've seen the glory of God,' John announces at the start of his gospel, and what follows is an account of Jesus walking the streets, sitting in homes, providing bread and fish and wine, and crouching on hillsides. God feeling pain, and hunger, and frustration at life's injustices. God cracking a smile at the comments and the funny mishaps. God with skin on. Not merely pretending to be human. That would never do. But one hundred percent rooted in life. In reality. Up close and personal. Sawdust in the creases of his palm. Dust in the frown furrows on his forehead. Grit in the laughter lines on his face.

### Beautiful

There's a lovely scene in the gospel series *The Chosen*, where Jesus is chatting with a group of curious children about his life and work, and as he talks he cleans his teeth. He's just woken up and is getting ready for the day. A little bleary at first, adjusting to the daylight, his mouth a tad dry from sleep perhaps. Because he was fully human. And so he cleans his teeth. Right there as he chats with the children. He experienced all these ordinary things. The children ask him if he has a favourite food and he says he likes many kinds of food. Especially bread. Which of course has great significance for him.

He used food all the time to help people connect with God. So they would remember the experience, and perhaps next time they ate bread and fish, or drank wine, they would be reminded and talk about Jesus. (And like the prophets he was unafraid to do unexpected and strange things because they would stick in people's heads.) Jesus asks the children if they know the prayer the Shema. They instantly begin to recite it, and Jesus is clearly entranced and moved as he hears them pray. I love his response when they have finished. He just says, 'Beautiful.'

It made me think that to Jesus prayers are never about prayers, songs are never about songs, liturgy is not about liturgy. Religion is never about religion, just as spirituality is not about spirituality. They are always about true love, and love is about God. Love in the fullest, most pure, most splendid, most gentle, most world-shaking, and most jaw-dropping sense. We may sometimes zip through prayers or songs we know well. Familiarity makes it hard not to do that. But love invites us to pause as we speak and sing, because there is more here. Always more. The prayers draw us closer, the liturgy nudges us towards mercy embracing truth, and the songs waken us once more to the presence of God. Even if we get the words wrong.

It really saddens me when getting to know Jesus is reduced to religion and haggling and arguments and criticism. I hate it. I'm sorry, I know hate is a strong word, but we so easily turn following this man of sorrow and joy, who changes lives every day, into something else, something smaller, something that misses the point. Jesus described following him as finding treasure in a field, so much treasure that nothing else compares. Nothing else! Jesus is the best news in the world, he's the person who can give us the affirmation and meaning and value and direction and compassion that we are all looking for, there is no one like him. It's not the easiest option but he never promised that.

74

**Treasure**

We walk into that room full of precious things only to discover it's become a den of rust, moths, and thieves. It's only as we turn and walk out again that we find treasure in another place entirely. The kind of treasure someone might well sell up and start again for, the kind of forever treasure that only grows in value.

(Based on Matthew chapter 6 verses 19-20.)

**The Man Who Fixed My Roof**

Jesus lived and worked in his local community, a small town of maybe a few hundred. He presumably knew popular songs of his day, as well as ancient songs and music passed down the generations. Music was vital to the first century Jewish communities as a way of keeping hope alive in a time of great difficulty and oppression. Little did the locals know that Jesus himself was going to be the way forward in the midst of all the pressure and despair. To them he was just another regular guy. Here's a little dialogue between two neighbours in Nazareth.

*I see you've finally got round to getting your roof fixed.*
Yea, the carpenter's been busy till now, he's popular.
*Seems to be doing a good job there.*
Yea, I'm very impressed.
*His dad not with him?*
No he's off at Sepphoris, got some jobs over there.
*Well, he's obviously coping on his own, when his old man retires he's got a job for life.*
Apparently not.

*What?*

He's leaving it soon, he says, handing the business to his brother Simeon.

*But he's the oldest boy! He's entitled.*

He says he's got other plans.

*Really? What else does a carpenter do?*

Build other things apparently. That's what he said.

*Other things?*

Yea, things that will last forever. I didn't get it really.

*Is he going into religion or something?*

Doubt it, doesn't seem the religious type to me. Mind you, he does talk about changing the world, and the one downfall he has is... hear that?

*He's stopped.*

Yea, probably spotted somebody and he's checking they're doing okay. Does that a lot. Thinks up a lot of stories too, he's very imaginative, says he's going to do something with them soon.

*Well, maybe he'll be a famous storyteller one day. Hey! And then you'll be able to say – see my roof – it was Jesus who fixed that.*

### Carpentry

Later, when Jesus began his ministry and word spread about him, I wonder how many people saw the carpentry work he'd done for them in a whole new light. And whether those repairs and crafted pieces would be signs for them, reminding them of him for the rest of their lives. Who could ever sit on a stool, notice the repaired leg, and not think on that extraordinary carpenter who also fixed the leg of the woman down the street.

### Lockdown

And on the subject of writing about life, and what we see around us, during the pandemic I had a go at scribbling this:

### That's Life In Lockdown

Another spring day, the sun is shining,
Streets so quiet, beaches empty,
Staying home now, safer that way,
Rainbows out and Easter trees glistening,
That's life in lockdown.

Up and down stairs raising money,
So many times it's just like Everest,
Round the garden a hundred times now,
A war-time hero outside raising millions,
That's life in lockdown.

Out the windows and on our doorsteps,
Clapping and cheering for our key workers,
So many faces on the front line,
So many heroes keeping things going now,
That's life in lockdown.

Two metres distance, masks and gloves on,
Smiling through and helping folks now,
Delivering food with bags on doorsteps,
Avoiding walkers, and dodging to the right and left,
That's life in lockdown.

Pubs are empty, cinemas shut now,
Zoom's the rage and split screen meetings,
Online quizzes, concerts, parties,
Long distance choirs all singing out their hearts now,
That's life in lockdown.

Soap and loo rolls all gone AWOL,
Pasta aisles strewn with tumbleweed,
Sanitiser's all the rage now,
Queuing outside with trolleys in the car park,
That's life in lockdown.

Full of questions about the future,
Nothing the same now, shifting landscapes,
Thank God for kindness and different thinking,
So much caring about one another now,
That's life in lockdown.

**Top ~~Five~~ Twelve New Wave Favourites**

*Rat Trap* (The Boomtown Rats)
*Whole Wide World* (Wreckless Eric)
*Another Girl, Another Planet* (The Only Ones)
*Dancing with Myself* (Generation X)
*Turning Japanese* (The Vapors)
*Because the Night* (Patti Smith)
*Is She Really Going Out With Him?* (Joe Jackson)
*Oliver's Army* (Elvis Costello)
*Cool for Cats/Up the Junction* (Squeeze)
*Do Anything You Wanna Do* (Eddie and the Hot Rods)
*Sound of the Suburbs* (The Members)

**Tears**

In November '79 we went as a family to stay with old friends of my parents in Chester. They lived in this wonderful large house, with two staircases, and a vast expansive garden. While there I bought Abba's *Arrival* and *The Album* on vinyl. Oh yes, I was still a diverse listener, punk may have been filling my airwaves, but I had plenty of space in the windmills of my mind for a whole glut of other groups and artists. I put on *Arrival* and played it over and over. I just couldn't get enough of tracks like *That's Me* and *When I Kissed the Teacher*. Those tunes burrowed into my brain and I just snuggled into them up there.

When we went to see *Mamma Mia! Here We Go Again* as a family, a couple of years ago, I found myself totally overwhelmed with emotion at the joy of an early scene in the school hall. Lily James takes the stage and breaks into singing that kissing the teacher number. It was an extraordinary experience, I've never had anything like it, the joy of the thing, the music, the exuberance. These all set me off. And the memories of first loving that song flooded over me again. I spent the whole film battling tears of happiness. I was glad we were sitting in the dark, though I worried the person next to me might be able to feel my seat wobbling whenever I shook a little with gentle sobbing.

It was a fabulous one-off experience of watching a film which just kept on bringing waterworks of joy. Afterwards I discovered my wife Lynn had felt the same, but not our girls. They loved the film and the songs but couldn't see what the blubbing was all about. 😊 (I was heartened to discover later that the respected film critic Mark Kermode had experienced something very similar. Great minds tear up alike. And anyway, who needs to apologise for crying in public, we quite readily laugh.)

### Hammer

In those vinyl-buying days I became rather protective of my growing album collection, I bought a load of plastic sleeves for them, to protect them from getting marked. I'm pedantic like that, have a phobia of grime and dirt. It's annoying. I'm grateful for the advent of online libraries and digital loans because it means I can borrow books without worrying about who has had them before me and whether they were making jam or eating croissants or doing the gardening as they read them. Terrible I know. I'm sorry to be so fussy like this. It's daft.

And it's odd because I grew up reading library books, those wonderful hardback novels, with those thick pages, packed with the adventures of William, and Lemon Kelly, and Jim Starling. And I had a stack of comic Annuals, most of which were probably second-hand. In the '90s I read a lot of the Fleming Bond novels out of the library. And another odd thing, I used to do street theatre regularly and I would end up sitting or lying on pavements and precincts which had been graced with goodness knows what. So I'm obviously conflicted re my aversion to grunge. (Grubbiness that is, not the music.)

We used to do a lot of robotic performance as a way of handing out our own homemade leaflets about our faith. We'd stand still and only move if someone took a leaflet. Quite effective as we found folks rarely threw them away, as they'd chosen to take them from us. We also used to mime to a host of songs. One particular piece sticks in the mind. We presented a two-person performance of the sacrifice and crucifixion of Jesus to Queen's *Hammer to Fall*. The power and punch of the song was perfect, and of course Freddy kept singing about the hammer falling, which is what happened when the Romans set about nailing people up. But the hammer fell on other things too as Jesus hung dying, not least on the poisonous sting of death itself. No longer an eternal curse. No longer a road to nowhere, but now a door thrown wide open to new life and peace with God. And having just mentioned street theatre...

**Top Weather-related Songs (there are lots)**
*Sunshine After the Rain* (Elkie Brooks – two for one there)
*The Sun Ain't Gonna Shine Anymore* (The Walker Brothers)
*I Can't Stand the Rain* (Eruption)
*Blowin' in the Wind* (Bob Dylan)
*Walking on Sunshine* (Katrina and the Waves)
*Storm in a Teacup* (The Fortunes)
*Thunder in my Heart* (Leo Sayer)
*Weather with You* (Crowded House)
*Wind of Change* (Scorpions)
*Cold as Ice* (Foreigner)
*Thunder Road* (Bruce Springsteen)
*Misty* (Ray Stevens)
*Fog on the Tyne* (Lindisfarne)

*Wind Beneath my Wings* (Bette Midler)
*The Flood* (Take That)
*Heatwave* (The Jam)
*Here Comes The Sun* (The Beatles)
*Mr Blue Sky* (ELO)

Some space for any thoughts, doodlings, scribblings, top fives, or musical memories of your own.

### Granddad's Bike

The night before I turned sixteen (Christmas Eve Eve 1978) I was sick. I started with a cold, went out carol singing (not on my own, with a group), came back and threw up. And mysteriously the cold went. Voom! I often wondered about that. But that's beside the point. My dad's birthday was on the 23rd December, the day before mine. And because I had a thing about throwing up, (experienced a lot of car sickness in my early days) I elected to stay up and sleep downstairs in a chair.

My dad had received a couple of albums for his birthday, the soundtrack to *Jesus Christ Superstar*, and *Night Gallery* by The Barron Knights, a group of cheeky chappies who were famous for spoofing pop songs. This collection featured *A Taste of Aggro* – a compilation which revisited Bony M's *Rivers of Babylon* ('There's a dentist in Birmingham...') and Brian and Michael's *Matchstalk Men* ('And he painted granddad's bike and next door's cats and dogs...'). I seem to recall listening to both these albums a lot over those days, and possibly through that night of affliction before my birthday.

To this day I love *Everything's Alright* and *Could We Start Again, Please.* (From *Superstar* not the Barron Knights.) *Everything's Alright* is about the moment when Mary anoints Jesus, but for me there's an echo of Jesus telling us not to worry about tomorrow. And to focus on today and the kingdom of God. I reckon that Jesus is very realistic about life, knowing that the uncertainty of tomorrow and the days after it, can turbocharge our anxiety. But God is here, and his name

84

is I Am, forever in the present moment. Right now, with you as you read this sentence. God in the today. And this is where he can help us and guide and strengthen us.

Another *Superstar* song *Could We Start Again, Please* is for those many moments when things take a wrong turn and plans go awry and we mess up again. In those moments it's never a bad thing to think of the parable of the Satnav: the kingdom of God is like a talking box which keeps guiding us back the way we need to be going...

### Bullocks

The day I left school, or the day I sat my last O' level, (one or the other), I came home to find three albums waiting in the hall for me. At that time (1979) my dad was working in the Ministry of Defence police patrolling the local airbase and EMI premises, and one of the perks about this was that he could buy music at a knock-down price. I told a guy at school this and he asked me if I could get an album for him. I agreed, but there was a snag. He wanted the infamous *Never Mind the Bullocks Here's the Sex Pistols*.

(#slightlytweakedtitlethere)

It's a shame that this wasn't the actual title because I'd have happily ordered it, but there was no way I could ask my dad for the real title. I felt bad, a bit of a failure, I never want to let anyone down. I wanted to get it for the guy at school, but instead I kept him hanging on for quite a while... before eventually plucking up the courage to admit it wasn't on the way.

Anyway, back to the end of my school days. Dr Feelgood's *Down by the Jetty*, The Eagles' *Hotel California*, and possibly Bruce Springsteen's *Born to Run* were waiting for me in the hall. My dad had ordered them for me and they arrived as I left school. A perfect way to finish my education. As I started to earn money I discovered there was a whole world of music out there now within my reach. When I got my first month's wages the first thing I did was go out and buy a hi-fi system for my room. Complete with wall mounted stereo speakers. I also bought a single by Bill Lovelady *Reggae for it Now*. I put it on and played it loud. A great feelgood song that fitted my mood perfectly. It felt like a new start, and the fulfilment of my dreams, all in one go. My own music machine.

### Rumours

Some time in the spring of 1980 my sister and I went to stay with a friend in Cornwall. We had lived there until the summer of '77, so we were catching up with old friends. But three unexpected things happened that weekend. Two of them were made of vinyl. My sister's friend had a couple of albums I listened to for the first time. One was *Monty Python Live at Drury Lane*. The other was *Rumours* by Fleetwood Mac.

Listening to them on repeat was not the most significant thing that happened during our brief stay, but these albums will always remind me of that weekend. Particularly *Rumours*. It was the start of a kind of love affair with Fleetwood Mac. And I still listen to them from time to time now. Recently Christine McVie died, and so that set me listening once more. I also really like an album she recorded with Lindsey Buckingham just a couple of years ago.

The other significant happening that weekend took place in Truro cathedral. I went with a group to hear the Christian writer and author David Watson. And at the end of the evening, as I sat in the pew just quietly worshipping God, I started to feel as if I were floating. The evening had been unemotional till then. No great whipping up of sensation or anything like that. And yet, as I sat with my head bowed thanking God for who he was, I felt something powerful begin to happen. It was my first encounter with what we call the power of the Holy Spirit. It was gentle, and affirming, and incredibly uplifting, and it signalled a new start in my life.

And I mention it here because this is life to me. A mixture of God and the ordinary. Vinyl records and the power of the Holy Spirit. All mixed up. One reminds me of the other. This is life. No separation. Perhaps one helps me hold onto the other. A divine reminder. *Rumours* is no more real than the encounter I had in the cathedral. Just as sheep could remind folks of the caring Shepherd who comes looking for them, so Fleetwood Mac and Monty Python can remind me of that unexpected meeting with the same generous God.

**Top ~~Five~~ Six Fleetwood Mac Favourites**
*Oh Diane*
*Little Lies*
*Yesterday's News* (from *Rumours)*
*Seven Wonders*

*Red Sun* (from *Buckingham McVie*)
*The Ledge* (from *Tusk)*

### Onslaught

The onslaught of punk rattled the music establishment, and even successful bands like Queen and Fleetwood Mac were tempted to have a go. Queen recorded the high energy *Sheer Heart Attack* and put it on their 1977 album *News of the World*. I came across it on the B-side of *Spread Your Wings*. I loved the raw, relentless punch of it, but had no idea at the time that the arrangement was a nod towards the punk invasion.

When Fleetwood Mac came to record their follow up to *Rumours*, Lindsey Buckingham had been listening to Talking Heads and The Clash and he was up for trying a different approach. The 1979 double album *Tusk* features several tracks with a faster, rougher sound. *The Ledge* and *That's Enough for Me* both come in around the two-minute mark. The LP contains a diverse mix of songs and much as I love *Rumours*, these days I'm more likely to put on *Tusk*. Not least because I'm less familiar with it. And when I say 'put on' *Tusk*, there is of course no vinyl or needle or cassette spooling involved. I just talk to a machine and hey presto.

### When Worlds Collide

*Rumours* came with a poster of Fleetwood Mac, I can still picture it now. It promptly went on my bedroom wall, joining Ian Dury, The Damned, Debbie Harry, The Police, and The Jam. Ian Durie had a union jack somehow clipped to his front teeth. Not a full-size flag, some sort of tiny brace thing. The Police picture had come in a copy of *Record Mirror*, a mid-page pull-out, but I didn't know who they were when I put it up. They looked cool. I wasn't actually much of a fan of The Damned, but they were plenty punky so up they went.

I know now they have the accolade of releasing the first ever punk single *New Rose*. It was produced by Nick Lowe, who had been a trailblazer in the early pub rock days with his band Brinsley Schwarz. Having trailblazed pub rock with his band, you could say he trailblazed punk as a producer. Having done their first single Nick Lowe also produced The Damned's first album, and Elvis Costello's first *five* albums, and Wreckless Eric's fine single *Whole Wide World*. He also wrote a protest song featuring one of life's great questions – (*What's So Funny 'Bout*) *Peace, Love, and Understanding*.

Punk was full of great protest songs, they may have been delivered with snarling, sweat and spit, but there was a genuine outcry within the sneers and sarcasm. The Clash particularly had plenty to say about inequality and injustice. And speaking of Mr Strummer, I may well have had The Clash up there blue-tacked to my wall but oddly I can't remember. My favourite band and I can't remember. And there were most likely other rebels up there too, I'm sure.

I still stick things up now. On my door here I have a new poster from Bruce's latest album *Only The Strong Survive*, it's up there along with a *Tintin* postcard, and a collection of small home-printed posters of favourite films. Including the brilliant *Jaws* and the wonderful *Sing Street*. Now that's a great fictional pop band story.

A group of '80s kids form a band and dress up like The Cure and Duran Duran in the process.

And with posters and artwork in mind, just yesterday I was messaging my best friend from school Jon, about our old art classes, and it reminded me of the time I made a right old mess on the page, just a mash of colour and splurge. My stroke of genius (so I thought) was to suddenly decide it looked like planets exploding and that it could have been a Queen album cover for a disc called *When Worlds Collide*. If there is an inspired idea there it's not in the artwork, it's surely in the idea that Queen would have made that album and called it that. My art teacher wasn't fooled. I got eight percent.

Also on my door is this poem wot I wrote for our younger daughter. It gives me an excuse to include it and give a moment's respite from all this pop music.

### Lucy and the Dragon

Lucy had a dragon,
With purple spikes and tufty hair.
It could fly and breathe out fire.
And snuggle in its dragon chair.

With bright green wings
And yellow feet, it was quite a sight,
It toasted pink marshmallows,
And flew her to the stars at night.

It told her tales of rescue,
Of princesses stuck in towers,
It flew her round the garden,

And made her laugh for hours.

On bonfire nights it lit the fire,
And warmed her in the cold,
On birthdays lit the candles,
And told her tales of old.

But it could not breathe out,
When they played out in the snow.
And if it coughed or sneezed,
All the snow would go!

Lucy loved the dragon,
And the dragon loved her too.
His tail made the perfect slide,
And down it Lucy flew.

The dragon was so big and strong,
But he was not a baddie.
When asked about the dragon's name,
Lucy just said, 'Daddy!'

Maybe one day it'll be a song.

**Truth**

Years later I learnt the true story behind *Rumours*.
When Fleetwood Mac began making their album all five
band members were having relationship problems, and
four of them, John and Christine, Lindsey and Stevie,
were actually couples in the band. And so they drew on
their splintering relationships for their songwriting.
Expressing the difficulties and pain.

Many of the tracks on that album are messages to one another. Admittedly some are more optimistic than others. Christine McVie's message to John McVie – *Don't Stop* perhaps has more hope about it than Lindsey Buckingham's message to Stevie Nicks – G*o Your Own Way.* But they found a way to express something real in those numbers. When the album was ready John McVie commented that it sounded like a bunch of rumours. Hence the name. Later Christine McVie said that when you listened to it through it sounded like something of a diary.

It was their most successful album, making them the biggest band in the world. I mentioned earlier that CS Lewis saying, 'If you want to be original, tell the truth.' Sometimes pain and trouble draw the truth from us, it's as if we feel we have less to lose, and it peels back the glossy layers on our life.

But it's not easy to be honest, especially in Christian circles, as you can feel the strange pressure of needing to look as if you have everything sorted. As if you have all the answers. Odd really when you look at the book of psalms which are full of guttural cries and ragged questions.

When I wrote the *Bloke's Bible* it was a kind of cry from the heart, or if not that, a spewing of the struggles I felt I was going through. It was a kind of therapy, and from some of the feedback I have had I think it has been useful for others. One of the verses from the Bible I thought on a lot was a line Jesus said, 'You will know the truth and the truth will set you free.' I can still be frightened by the truth, but when I dare find a way to share it sometimes others feel they can join in too.

It was easier back then, in the middle of a muddle, when I felt frustrated and angry and lost, to express the questions and complaints and clouds. Bono, of the band U2, once said that he figured smack in the middle of a contradiction is a good place to be. We all live smack in the middle of contradictions.

I believe in peace but am often not peaceful. I believe in love but am often selfish. I believe in hope but swing between despair and trust, sometimes a hundred times a day. I take a lot of comfort and encouragement from Leonard Cohen's lines from his song Anthem, in which he sings about the light coming into us through the cracks in our lives.

Good old letter-writing Paul said something similar in his second note to the Corinthians chapter 4. 'We're all cracked pots, damaged vessels, and it's the light of God that shines out of us.' In John chapter 4 Jesus promised a hurting woman at a well that living water would leak out of her, and it sure did when she ran back to tell everyone about it.

Leaks and cracks, we don't have to be strong to be used by God. 'Blessed are you when you are at the end of your rope...' so says Jesus in The Message version of the Bible. A friend just mentioned this to me now in a conversation. These are profound truths, but painful ones too. We don't want to be weak, or cracked, or at the end of ourselves.

This is where songs and stories can be so useful, because we can tell the truth wrapped in a tune and a tale. So others can hopefully find themselves in those chronicles of contradiction. I'm sure that's why Jesus used so many stories about this otherworldly way of life, so we might see ourselves reflected in his tales and want to join in, becoming real life bumbling characters in his new kingdom.

'We long to be perfect, strong, and right,
But it's not about us, it's about the light
Of God coming in through the cracks,
Light that shines in and out through the gaps.'

### Top Five Favourite U2 Songs
*One*
*I Still Haven't Found What I'm Looking For*
*Sweetest Thing*
*Stuck in a Moment*
*Who's Gonna Ride Your Wild Horses*

### Tubthumping
I have always loved the song *Tubthumping* by Chumbawamba, though it was recorded in the '90s it harks back to those heady punk days. But it's not just a song these days, for me it's about my friend Justin too. In the noughties, whilst working as part of the Lee Abbey Community at the Conference Centre in Devon, we often held discos and when *Tubthumping* came on, Justin and I used to leap around like mad. It was a brilliant, explosive experience.

I've never been very good at dancing, but I find a freedom in it. I've danced a lot over the years.

94

Chaotically. Happily. Mostly on my own. Dancing with others usually cramps my style. I feel free when I really dance and forget others. Sometimes dancing can be about trying to impress, or look cool, or get the moves right. And that never works for me. It kills it.

But dancing with Justin to *Tubthumping* is different. The last time we leapt around together was at his wedding in Virginia. A great time. Hot and sweaty and me in a hired suit that was just a little too big. Brilliant.

I still have bursts of joy too, dancing in our kitchen with Lucy, our younger daughter, at the time of writing she is nine. I do recall a lovely moment when The Specials came on with their song *Message to You Rudy* and we jumped around and boogied to it. Boogieing. Now that shows my age. I don't think people do that anymore. But enough – on with the book.

### Skin

In the movie *The Last Temptation* Jesus goes to a party and dances. I love that. And I had not seen it portrayed before. But of course Jesus would have danced. Jewish men did that. And Jesus went to plenty of parties. And I'm sure he had a great time. It's just one of the many things Jesus did we don't often think, talk or sing about.

I mentioned earlier the scene in the series *The Chosen,* when Jesus meets a group of children and he sits there cleaning his teeth. They have woken him up and so, a little bleary, he needs to get ready for the day. Jesus cleaning his teeth and then the children reciting the Shema perfectly captures the word made flesh, or

God with skin on. Teeth and talking to God. No separation. It's all part of life.

And so, returning to dancing for a moment, and the freedom that Jesus can bring, here's a little poem wot I wrote when I spied a couple of folks dancing on a bridge in our home town.

### Dancing
I saw a couple dancing on a bridge,
Making up moves as they went,
Not some poster Manhattan skyline view,
With the sun dying behind them,
Lighting the scene with other-worldly rays,
But here, in my home town,
As dog walkers and shoppers meandered past.
You don't see that too often,
Celebration and liberty sublimely oblivious,
Who cares how it looks to others,
Life is for living and dancing is free,
And you never know when
Someone like me is watching,
And feeling better because they were there.

### Top Five Dancing Songs
*Tubthumping* (Chumbawamba)
*Dancing in the Moonlight* (Toploader)
*Sit Down* (James)
*Come on Eileen* (Dexy's Midnight Runners)
*September* (Earth Wind and Fire)

**In the Quiet of the Night**

And thinking of Jesus full of life and true humanity, I thought I'd include this piece. An imagined conversation between Jesus and Mary in Bethany, only days before he will give his life for us.

It's getting late, the others have all turned in, there is the faint sound of background snoring. Just him and Mary now, Martha busied herself for a while tidying up, but she's exhausted herself too.

He can still smell the distinctive scent in the air, that perfume will litter the atmosphere for a long time yet. He glances at her, she smiles back. He can tell there are questions in her mind, words she is longing to let fall from her lips.

'What is it really like?' she whispers, afraid perhaps of asking it. 'Being you?'

He looks at his hands, sees the years of making things.

'In many ways it's not unlike being you,' he says, 'lonely at times, frustrated, misunderstood...'

She glances at him, looks at that face she is growing to love.

'And funny too, of course,' he says. 'What is life without laughter, and wonder, surprise and discovery?'

'But you're not just like me are you?' she says. 'And you're not like Peter and James are you?'

He looks back at her, holds her gaze for a while.

'I love being human,' he says, 'never knew it before. I mean, yes, we knew the mechanics of it... but being on the inside. Being decked out with all this skin and these emotions. I love that. Most of the time.'

97

Silence. She frowns and looks away, so now it's his turn to study her.

'You're right,' he says eventually. 'There's an ache. Inside. I have so much to do and say, so much I've seen and known. But it's too much. And so I have to carry it alone. It's why I slip away in the dark hours each morning. I talk to my father about it all. I love the breaking dawn, love the world waking again, love the little moments and the sounds and the colours and the smells.'

'You're not going to tell me are you?' Suddenly there is an edge to her voice, as if he's upset her.

He knows, he knows why she has suddenly thrown this verbal jab. They lock eyes again. And so much passes between them, so much that is left unsaid.

'I sometimes feel like a little child,' he says, 'playing, loving life, offering new discoveries to my friends, exploring a very big world. And then I wonder if I can do all that I need to do. Fragile like this. But at other times I feel like a giant, looking down on creation, seeing how it all works and the bits that are broken. The people who struggle to fit in. And I know how they feel, because I feel too big to fit in myself, because of all I'm carrying.'

'And me? Do you see me?' And her face says it all, her longing to be truly known. And more.

He nods. 'Always,' he says, 'always.'

### Known and Seen

In the book of Genesis (chapter 16) Hagar runs away. She's pregnant and things are not going well for her. So she ups and offs, but she meets an angel who talks with her for a while and tells her to go back. As she returns she gives God a name – El-roi – it means *the God who sees me*. The God who knows and understands us, and our situations. The characters in both *Avatar* films talk about seeing each other. For them it's a mark of respect and understanding. We can feel very overlooked in society. Invisible at times. We are never invisible to God. Never. He sees us. He cherishes us. Always.

Some space for any thoughts, doodlings, scribblings, top fives, or musical memories of your own.

**Suits**

In November 1979 another band inspired by the times appeared in black and white suits, dancing to edgy reggae, and with their own record label. They had reworked an old Prince Buster song, *Al Capone,* and so here was Terry Hall singing about *Gangsters* in his inimitable bored and angry style. 2-Tone had arrived.

Jerry Dammers from Coventry founded his own record label and he and the Specials took the charts by storm. He signed other bands – The Beat, The Selecter, The Bodysnatchers and Madness. The music was punk-infested ska, and their intent was obvious. To unite people and get them dancing. Their first album was like nothing I'd heard before.

Madness soon moved on to a bigger label, and became one of the biggest bands of the '80s, but 2-Tone went on, and for a while it brought a whole different vibe. I loved the outfits, the lean mean look, the punky reggae sound, but mostly the catchy tunes. The upbeat melodies.

Over the next two years The Selecter released one album, while The Beat released a couple. The Specials had two number one singles, two albums and an EP. They burned bright for two years, ending their reign with the haunting *Ghost Town*. Then three of them slipped away, formed Fun Boy Three and helped launch Bananarama, while The Beat became Fine Young Cannibals. By then the 2-Tone uprising was mostly over. Meanwhile, something else extraordinary was happening. The Jam were at number one. What??!

**Top ~~Five~~ ~~Six~~ Seven Ska Favourites**

*Gangsters* (The Specials)
*Message to You Rudy* (The Specials)
*Do Rock Steady* (The Bodysnatchers)
*Tears of a Clown* (The Beat)
*Do Nothing* (The Specials)
*The Bed and Breakfast Man* (Madness)
*Enjoy Yourself* (The Specials)

### Jumpers

A while ago I caught some clips from an episode of Top of the Pops in 1977, and it made me realise why Punk and New Wave caused such a stir in the late '70s. Top of the Pops was done in a certain way, with a particular look, a particular way of dancing, presented in a particular tone of voice. And millions of us watched. The likes of Leo Sayer, Showaddywaddy, Pan's People and Manhattan Transfer, kept us glued to that goggle box on a Thursday night.

Cut to The Jam, on the same programme, with their debut single *In the City* – and suddenly we're talking something very different. Different attitude, different language, different style of presentation, different way of approaching things altogether. Paul Weller and his mates were not dancing in the same way, not singing in the same way, they had anger and passion and they cared about their lyrics. They were tired of the old ways and they were out there to make something contrary happen. When you compare the two styles you can see why this new attitude was so revolutionary, the scene was set for a battle between the old and the new.

I loved the suits The Jam wore and would have happily bought one to wear to work in the bank, if only I'd had a little more nerve and a tad more oomph. But really it was the tunes I loved, and the energy of their performance, and Paul Weller's attitude in his tight-lipped vocals.

### One

And here they were at number one. How could that have happened? These were the upstarts from Woking, the whippets in suits who spat their lyrics and pogoed two feet in the air. Music for mavericks. Now everybody was starting to like them.

And it wasn't as if they'd sold out. *Going Underground* is typical of The Jam sound, aggressive, punchy, anti-establishment stuff. It doesn't have a disco beat and it isn't a revamp of an old classic. And there it was, Toppermost of the Poppermost, to quote John Lennon. I couldn't believe it. Somehow, when I wasn't looking, The Jam had made it big.

The Clash hadn't. Not in that way. They were making great albums, but inevitably heading for disintegration. And the Sex Pistols were long gone. Stiff Little Fingers made it into the top twenty, but that was it. The Jam would go on to have four number one singles. It was ridiculous. Extraordinary. Unthinkable.

### Lent

And thinking of The Jam on Top of the Pops inevitably makes us think of Lent. Of course it does. Because there are obvious similarities. Those forty days of desert in

Matthew chapter 4 meant that Jesus was in a time of change, he was moving from being the local builder-carpenter who could fix your house and mend that table, to being a radical teacher who would shake the world to its absolute core.

He was not going to dance, sing, act or speak in quite the same way as anyone else, and that required preparation. He was changing, and he needed forty days alone to do that. To face himself, sort out his priorities and get well-grounded. He was about to make something different happen. A *new wave* kind of challenge to the way people lived, a *punk* explosion to their understanding of life. A different attitude, a different language, a different way of being entirely. Passion, anger and energy.

Something very different was coming about in that wilderness. People couldn't be the same again.

### Outer Space

One of the memorable comments made in the documentary *Punk Britannia* comes from Mark Perry, who in true punk spirit started his own magazine, or fanzine, called *Sniffin' Glue*. He says that, though he was a punk, he still had Deep Purple albums... it's easy to forget, but the punks hadn't come from outer space... Johnny Rotten might have proclaimed punk a ground zero of music, but they were all shaped by previous bands and songs. They may not have been listening to Billy Joel and the Bee Gees as I was, but they were steeped in the pop and rock culture of the '60s and '70s.

Sex Pistol Glen Matlock says that he drew on Abba's *SOS* when he wrote *Pretty Vacant*, and Elvis Costello was inspired by *Dancing Queen* when he put *Oliver's Army* together. Apparently he and his band the Attractions were listening to Abba's *Greatest Hits volume two* as they drove round in their tour van. (I believe Elvis's dad sang on the old R White's Lemonade advert about being a secret lemonade drinker.)

The Sex Pistols would release their own versions of Eddie Cochran's *C'mon Everybody* and *Somethin' Else*. The Ramones even covered Cliff Richard's *Do You Wanna Dance.* And without a hint of irony. They really didn't come from outer space. We are all influenced by what is around. Only God can think of a brand-new colour, we have to mix and blend what is already here.

### Legs & Co

Viewers of Top of the Pops witnessed a strange and glorious moment in the summer of 1980 when dancers Legs & Co (successors to Pan's People) danced to *Bankrobber* by The Clash. In their own inimitable style. The Clash refused to appear on Top of the Pops so with their single riding high in the top twenty something had to be done. Enter Legs & Co dressed as er... yes... bank robbers, complete with stripy shirts, hankies over their faces and swag bags. Fantastic. And it's a great example of the culture crash, the old and the new colliding and mixing together. A truly strange combination.

When The Clash sent in their 'Awfully sorry, can't make it in today' note, they surely never imagined this. Their reggae-punk classic about daddy busting banks writ large in this *Seaside Special* pre-punk way. Not at all in the spirit of rebellion. *Clashing*, you might say.

Jesus commented on this kind of clash, using wine skins and clothes as examples. He said something along the lines of, 'Trying to bring in the new can be tricky and awkward, it can result in a strange and unsettling mix that often makes a mess. People prefer the old to the new,' he said, 'so they try and hang onto bits of both, but trying to put the two together can cause accidents.'

A new way forward required a new mindset, not just a change of socks, but a whole new outfit. And more than that, to stretch the analogy, a whole new heart. As Ezekiel predicted in chapter 11 of his epic book, hearts of stone would be transplanted and replaced with hearts of flesh, hearts that beat to the rhythm of another drum. Spirits that would connect with the spirit of God.

Unthinkable before that dusty carpenter emerged from the desert, his mind set on you and me. And I can't resist a reference here to Blondie's heart of glass, which turned out to be brittle and hard. Ezekiel was singing from a new hymn sheet about truly human hearts infused with life and kindness, tuned to the ways of God.

### A Punk Top Five
*Sheena is a Punk Rocker* (The Ramones)
*Germ Free Adolescents* (X-Ray Specs)
*Boredom* (Buzzcocks)
*Something Else* (The Sex Pistols)
*Love Song* (The Damned)

**Changes**

As the 1980s picked up speed something appalling and unthinkable happened. Punk and New Wave began to fade, making way for synth pop and the New Romantics. Ripped jeans and safety pins gave way to flouncy outfits, big hair, and an explosion of eye makeup. What was going on? I was sidewhacked by this other-worldly invasion. People say that seeing Bowie sing *Starman* on Top of the Pops was disturbing, well, my *Starman* moment came when Boy George appeared singing *Do You Really Want to Hurt Me*. The world was shifting again. It was startling and unsettling. But not all of it. I did like some of the new stuff.

Gary Numan and his Tubeway Army took everyone by surprise by having a huge number one with *Are Friends Electric*, a dark and brooding film noir epic. I found that song enthralling. Gary Numan now says he'd intended to record a punk album, but found a synthesiser in the studio. Many of these new flouncy pop stars had grown up with punk and were inspired by it. I also liked Depeche Mode with their *New Life* and *Just Can't Get Enough* singles. And Visage's *Fade to Grey* was captivating too. I bought *Tainted Love* by Soft Cell. And Ultravox's epic *Vienna* album.

Midge Ure had already blazed a musical trail in the '70s with the band Slik, having a number one with *Forever and Ever*, then going on to front Rick Kids with ex-Sex Pistol Glen Matlock, before singing lead on Visage's *Fade to Grey*. He was a busy guy and would later have a solo number one with *If I Was*. But before then, while still in Ultravox in '84, he would write and produce *Do They Know It's Christmas?* with old Boomtown Rat, Bob Geldof. A story that has inspired me ever since Lynn and I caught a ten-year retrospective on Radio One in 1994.

Bob had seen Michael Buerk's news report from Ethiopia and felt he had to do something. So he called up his New Romantic mate and they got together to merge a couple of their song ideas. Then Bob got on the blower and strong-armed a load of A-list popsters to make it down to the studio on a forthcoming Sunday morning. On the day it was getting late and Boy George hadn't turned up so they phoned him in New York and told him to get on Concorde quick! There was no stopping Bob. He was all-guns blazing to do something to help.

We're used to celebrity charity singles now, but back then this was a whole new page in pop history. And Bob wasn't taking no for an answer. When the government refused to waive the VAT on the single Bob cornered PM Maggie Thatcher and wouldn't let up until the government agreed to donate to the charity the same amount they'd taken in tax. The morning after recording, after being up all night mixing the song, Bob raced to Mike Read's Radio One breakfast show to announce the release of the single.

To paraphrase a line from the film *Raiders of the Lost Ark* – 'You and I are passing through history, this *is* history.' There is something about Geldof's drive here, willing to go all out for something he knew was important, something he believed in. And he was willing to try something new, something no one had thought possible before. I'll never do anything on this scale of course, but there are still things out there, ideas that the great Sower is sowing, waiting for them to take root in our lives to bring the world some good, and hope and light.

One of my favourite sayings comes from Shane Claiborne – 'Get ready because God is preparing you for something very, very… small. Because it's small things that change the world.' Who knows what small ideas are heading our way right now. Hovering in the ether, waiting for us to notice them as they settle in the quiet corners of our minds and souls.

### Changes Two

And that said, back to the early '80s music scene. I may have been into Ultravox and a few other new bands, but Spandau Ballet wrongfooted me. Duran Duran too. I wasn't sure about The Human League, though I did like *The Sound of the Crowd*. And as catchy as *Karma Chameleon* was, things clearly weren't the same any more. Those guitar bands were in the rear-view mirror. It was blatantly unfair. The short sharp songs were being drowned out.

The Clash did bring out their 1980 opus *Sandinista*. A strange and diverse and at times wonderful triple album. Thirty-six songs on one LP! And that only a year after their nineteen tracks on *London Calling*. But I only liked about half of them. (Which let's face it still makes for an eighteen-track album).

Joe and the boys had discovered America and were quite happy to let the influences show. They even put a rap track on the new album. *Magnificent Seven*. It's often cited as a great song, but you know... it's rap. It's talking rather than singing. I can't hear the tune. *Sandinista* opened with that but then was thankfully followed by *Hitsville UK*, which is full of tune and melody and hooky catchiness.

The album also included *Washington Bullets*, *Somebody Got Murdered, Police on my Back* and *Something about England*. All great songs. But there were strange dub versions of songs too, the style was probably cutting edge and bang up to date, I just wasn't into all that. Not long after I got *Sandinista* I recorded the tracks I liked and gave the LP to a friend in the bank. Not only were the times a-changing. The Clash were too. And so was I.

### Top 5 New Romantic/Synth Favourites
*Ashes to Ashes* (David Bowie)
*New Life* (Depeche Mode)
*Vienna* (Ultravox)
*Are Friends Electric* (Tubeway Army)
*Only You* (Yazoo)

### Ready Bready Fish
Before he was out making his home wherever he laid his hat, Paul Young was singing in the Streetband about munching on *Toast*. Yes. Really. They had a hit with a song about cooked bread. It was happy and fun, and made you want to reach for the *Mothers Pride*. Other bakers are available. And with bread in mind, here's an old episode of *Ready Bready Fish*...

Presenter: So Jesus, welcome to *Ready Bready Fish,* really excited to have you on, we've heard lots about you, walking on water and all that. And I see you have a bag full of goodies there, so open it up and let's see what you have for us today. Ah right, a couple of fish, that's a good start, and... five little loaves. Yes, lovely, what's next? Nothing? That's it – you've nothing else?

Well what are you going to do with this? Make a fishy bread and butter pudding perhaps? Could work. No. You're going to serve it just like this. Bread and fish. Fish and bread. Well that's nothing special. We expect miracles on this show you know, you need to turn it into something extraordinary. No? Still can't be persuaded.

What are you doing now, you want that basket, okay, and then... what next... say a prayer? We're all saying a prayer right now, I can promise you that Jesus. (Bows head, then looks up) Anything happened? Has it turned into salmon and smoked chowder or gourmet seafood paella maybe? Nope ok. What? Hand them out, to this lot? We've got a hefty audience here Jesus, and the crew eat like velociraptors I can tell you. This won't go far.

Okay then. But on your head be... oh... wait a minute... where did this lot come from, er... can we get some help here... I can't carry it all, I'm gonna drop it... I need lots of help with all this fish... yes! Now, grab that basket, and that one... oh my goodness! How did you do it? Where did you get all this from? We've got too much now, we'll be collecting the leftovers all afternoon. Marvellous! Unbelievable! Never seen anything like it on this show before, I can tell you. Genius.

111

Mind you, they're all looking a bit thirsty now. Don't suppose you brought any wine Jesus... you don't happen to make your own do you?... What's that? You have more bread? Well I think we have more than enough already! What? You? Follow you? Living bread? Oh... Er... I'm not sure... that's a bit unexpected. Hmm. I'll get back to you on that one...

### Learning
I find myself in a place where I want to discover new ways of communicating what is in the Bible. Like pop music, I want to keep moving forward. And not just for the sake of it, not at all, but because I want to help people experience the reality and help, the compassion and purpose that are wrapped up in the good news of Jesus.

Jesus was constantly inventive, still is, he used all kinds of things to help people connect with their God, he didn't just tell them things, he invited them in, got them to experience stuff, food, water, fish, wine, he wanted them to learn with their hands as much as with their heads.

Twenty-odd years ago DJ Fatboy Slim threw a free party on the beach at Brighton. Sixty thousand people were expected. In the end nearly a quarter of a million pitched up. There was fear in the air, would there be unrest? A riot even? Not at all. A quarter of a million people had a good time. It makes me wonder whether the friends of Jesus were a bit worried when they saw the size of the crowd and heard the collective stomachs rumbling in Matthew chapter 14. Would there be

112

trouble? Unrest with so many people dissatisfied and hungry?

'You feed them,' Jesus said when his mates pitched up complaining about the size of the crowd. And their jaws must have hit the floor. How could they do that? Of course, Jesus didn't really mean they had to do it alone, but he wanted them to join in. He was about to demonstrate the generous, welcoming, counter-cultural kingdom of God. He was about to make way too much food for everyone, he needed help. And they would never forget the experience. It was what we call kinaesthetic learning. Hands-on, tactile, learning through doing. Not just for a few, for everyone.

And when he did talk to folks he was always telling them stories, stories about things they would go off and do. Stories about mending clothes, pouring wine, losing sheep, sowing seeds. They would do these things and remember, they would do these things and see what Jesus was meaning. Not hypothetical stories, not theory, but practice.

We live in a world where more and more people are delivering sermons. They may just be a few lines long on Twitter, but we are being told what to think time and again. We cannot possible remember or apply all the good advice.

So how can we help people better engage with the words of life? Especially if they quickly forget what they hear, or don't want to read lots of stuff? How can we join in with the invitation, 'You feed them?'

I've just noticed that I say more about this on pages 134 and 135. So I'll leave it there for now. This is a good place for a blank page though, for your own reactions and comments and talkback.

Some space for any thoughts, doodlings, scribblings, top fives, or musical memories of your own.

### The Gap

On their 1978 Album, just called *The Album*, Abba sang about the hole in your soul, and how it has to be rock'n'roll that fills it. Rock'n'roll, hole in your soul, rhymes well. But I always had misgivings about the track. There is no doubt a gap inside us all, but I doubt that any kind of music is the right shape to fully fill it. Pete Greig in his book *Dirty Glory* describes the way we often try and fill the gap inside with stuff that only makes the gap bigger. This is how advertising works. Buy this product and you'll be satisfied. Until you see the next billboard with the same promise on it.

By 1981 I had got into a habit of buying music regularly, I had disposable income from working in the National Westminster Bank (you were arrested if you simply called it NatWest back then), and at some point I reached a level where I was sometimes barely getting to know one album before thinking about buying the next one. Sir Cliff, the artist formerly known as er... Cliff, took a different stance from Abba. When he entered Eurovision for the second time, he sang *Power to All our Friends*. (Any guesses as to what he sang the first time?) This song featured a line about the folk who gave us rock'n'roll and in doing so made life complete. But he took issue with that line, and instead sang about how rock'n'roll had made life so sweet.

I guess for a while I was looking for rock'n'roll to fill the hole in my soul. And no album was ever perfect. Nothing ever hit that sweet spot. And so it was, that in the winter of 1981, after my second holiday at the Lee Abbey Christian Community and Conference Centre in

North Devon, I decided to give up what I saw as secular music. That is, music that was not specifically Christian. I felt it was a similar call to the one Jesus gave to the rich young ruler in Luke chapter 18, when he asked him to give up everything and follow him. The young ruler's riches meant too much and would only get in the way. For me it was music. I needed to step away. And so from 1982 to 1988 I bought practically no chart music. I gave some of my collection away and destroyed some I felt was too dark. It may seem an extreme thing to do, but my focus had shifted, everything in me had changed and it felt the right thing to do at that time.

And it did me a lot of good, and freed me to see pop music in a different light. It was all about the place of secular music in my life at that time. I realise now that, though music can never satisfy that hole inside, it often illuminates the gap and sometimes points towards what can satisfy it. I also now see music as music, without that sacred/secular divide. Mostly anyway. But perhaps I'm able see it like that precisely because I stepped away from it for a while.


### God Gave Rock'n'Roll

In 1973 Argent sang *God Gave Rock & Roll to You*, assuring the world that he put it in the soul of everyone. I do concur with that. Not least because it recognises a gift and a giver. It's easy to confuse the two, I guess we all do that from time to time. The Christian band Petra covered the song on their 1984 *Beat the System* album. (So that surely means it's an acceptable song 😊!) That's where I first came across it. And though not everyone will applaud the message, music is the great gift which expresses so much, whether on a Fender Stratocaster or a church organ. Even perhaps possibly... on the bagpipes? (Feel free to discuss.)

### Desperate

Back in those early banking days I had started drinking too much. From time to time I would have a night out with others from the bank, when we would hit a pub and then go on to a local night club, Mr B's. It was the end of the '70s, and the brave new dawn of the '80s. The era of disco, and the likes of Chic and Sister Sledge, Earth Wind and Fire and The Village People. I was no great dancer, but I was of an age when I no doubt thought I was. I have always been a shy country boy, and I found that a few glasses of amber nectar helped me overcome my fear of embarrassment. Though having done that I most likely increased the chances of embarrassing myself.

This lifestyle hit a wall though when I tried to organise a night out with a couple of friends and no one turned up. After a few drinks alone in the pub, getting increasingly annoyed, I called a couple of my mates (I still remember the barman giving me a wary look as I was clearly unhappy) and they took pity on me and came out. But it was a sign of the times really, I was veering off course, and desperate for a better way in life. The following day, hungover, I went with my parents for my second visit to that place called Lee Abbey.

## China Shop

After years of believing in and reading about and relating to God (and to some degree hanging about on the side-lines, a reserve on the bench) I had a powerful experience and a profound encounter with him though my two visits to Lee Abbey in Devon. The two visits were a year apart, and the first one six months after the experience in Truro Cathedral, and it's a sign of how much patience God has that inbetween the two visits I carried on my own sweet and ill-advised way.

But after that second visit my relationship with God took on a vibrancy and reality, coming alive in a whole new way. I think he'd spent years nudging me towards this and everything changed in the autumn of 1981. (I still have plenty of times when I retire to the bench though and need nudging back into play.) I caused quite a stir in the bank after I came alive again, instead of hiding my faith under a banknote, I started unleashing it on everyone, and I guess the image of a bull in a china shop comes to mind. I was suddenly inspired and motivated and had to learn how to harness all that in the best way. Mind you, there are times now when I feel I've harnessed that bull far too much. It never even gets to run loose in the field now, never mind the china shop.

I mentioned earlier that I have been reading Bono's autobiography *Surrender* (having finished Nick Hornby's study of *Prince and Dickens*). In it he freely admits that if asked to give his life to Jesus in a coffee shop today he'd be on his feet again. I love his approach to that. Every day can be a day of giving our lives to Jesus. The biggest learning curve, the neverending embrace. Bono also mentions bringing Jesus into everything he's done, including the banal and the profane.

I guess I'm trying to do a little of that in this book, remind myself of God with me in everything. There is no separation between the spiritual and the ordinary to God, no line dividing the religious and the regular. Life is life. And when I'm in church and singing a worship song I'm still that guy who eats too much chocolate and listens to raucous punk.

### Christians

My good friend Simeon has recently given me another Bono quote, 'Christians are hard to tolerate I don't know how Jesus does it!' And that reminds me of a quote that used to be stuck on one of the walls in the youth office at Lee Abbey. 'There must be something in this Christianity, it's survived two thousand years of Christians!'

### Spiritual Punk

I discovered that there was a burgeoning Christian pop music scene, and I have fond memories of my first visit to a Christian bookshop in Bristol, when I came away with four Christian albums. Bands like Moral Support, The Barret Band and Petra became staples in my life. And on the first record buying trip I got a couple of discs by singer Don Francisco, a great bible storyteller. He brought the good book to life in his songs, and I played them repeatedly. I also found an album called Sing Good News, a collection of songs drawing on the text of the Good News Bible. Brilliant. To this day I can still quote bits of that Bible because of the songs.

I also found that there were one or two pseudo-punk bands, The Predators come to mind. But there wasn't much out there. I guess Christianity and punk are not easy mosh-pit mates. At times when I mention loving '70s rock, I find there are only a few Christians who loved punk as I did. To be honest I reckon that punk and Christianity have loads in common. Punk was about a DIY mentality. Having a go, making a start, not needing to be good enough. And if there's one thing you see in the Bible, it's that Jesus was daily inviting people to make a start. Take a step, have a go and see where it took them. It isn't about being a Good Christian, it's about learning from your mistakes.

I also reckon that praying is spiritual punk, because you cannot control it, people pray in all kinds of ways, in all kinds of places, with all kinds of words. And though we might say tidy and organised prayers at church and in meetings, the gut-centred cries we pour out to God when alone are not unlike some of those yelps the punk bands were emitting at times. And anyone can do it. Atheists, agnostics, amateurs. Well, I guess we're all amateurs when it comes to praying. I once heard a monk from Taizé say that we're not invited to get good at praying, we're just invited to do it.

**Top ~~Five~~ Ten Favourite Christian Songs**

*Witch Hunt* (Petra)
*Whole world* (Petra)
*Denomination Blues* (77s)

*Voice on the Wind* (Petra)
*Voice in the Night* (Barratt Band)
*He's Alive* (Don Francisco)
*20ᵗʰ Century* (Moral Support)
*Cyan City* (Moral Support)
*All at Sea* (Phil and John)
*When I First met Jesus* (The Housemartins)

### 68 Guns

I did buy albums by the then upcoming U2. I had heard they were Christians, and I ended up with their first five albums. Like so many other bands of the time they were inspired by punk and in particular The Ramones. I have been reading more of Bono's autobiography *Surrender* and I was amazed and heartened to read that to this day the group pray before every show. (So we have punk and prayer now.) One of the biggest bands in the world. Inspired by an album that was less than half an hour in length. A band that has faith. And a clear vision of themselves, knowing they can be pretentious and overblown, and honest about who they are.

I later got into The Alarm too, they seemed to have echoes of The Clash about them, the same fierce fury, and most importantly, the tunes were good. *68 Guns*, and *Where Were You Hiding When the Storm Broke* were singalong anthems without a shadow of a doubt. And again I had heard they had Christianity in their DNA, particularly Mike Peters, the lead singer. I also read Christian meaning into their lyrics. Whether intended or not. Particularly one track *The Deceiver*.

When I went to Greenbelt Christian rock festival in 1986 I had the unexpected joy of wandering into a tent late on Saturday night to find Mike Peters tuning up with a scratch band. I had inadvertently tripped over an impromptu Alarm-style gig. It was fantastic. My experience of Greenbelt in general was not so great, I wasn't in the happiest of places, (I was in a mood all weekend) and the experience was a shock to the system. I was living and working at Lee Abbey at the time, and that was a gentler community compared to the creative edge of the arts festival. It was also rainy. Not brilliant when you're camping and you only have a makeshift tent. I do remember wandering around in the dark (literally and metaphorically) and coming across a rabble of a punk band on an outdoor stage. There must have been about fifteen folks and a dog, crammed onto a circular bandstand. Can't remember the kind of noise they made, or how long they made it for, but I seem to remember enjoying them.

I always love watching buskers, I feel a certain affinity with them, having done a lot of street-theatre myself. I try and give them a few minutes of my time, and occasionally a few coins from my pocket. I know how hard it is to grab The General Public. Especially those intent on shopping or walking through your stage area. I'm all for entertaining the troops on the sidewalk. We have seen a guy over at Westward Ho! a couple of times, singing old '70s numbers with a karaoke machine. He raises money for the NHS, and as soon as I heard him singing *Back of My Hand* by The Jags I knew I had to stop and give him some time.

**The End**

In 1981 I passed my driving test. One of my abiding memories of that day is of taking the car out on my own for the first time that evening, and almost scraping another car as I squeezed through a gap that was really too small. And hearing Billy Joel on the radio singing *Say Goodbye to Hollywood* from his *Songs in the Attic* live album. Of course I was listening to the radio, how could I drive without the radio on?

A few years later I was watching a video of a Bruce Springsteen concert with some friends. He began to improvise a story about being out in his car and the thing falling to bits little by little. But it wasn't a problem, no matter how bad things got, he still kept going. Nothing could stop him. Until the worst happened. The radio died. That was the end. There was no going on. It seemed to me Bruce had his priorities right.

I bought my first car, a Renault Four, from a friend in the bank, and having passed my test the next vital thing of course was being able to play my music in the thing. Roll on Christmas when I got a cassette player that flipped over when it reached the end of side one. My dad fixed a speaker to the wall of each footwell and I was off. Did I have an MOT? No idea mate, but I can play you this Billy Joel cassette without having to take it out and turn it over.

Nowadays music in a moving vehicle has moved on drastically. We had our current car three years before we realised we could plug a USB stick into the system and play a million billion hours of music. For years our older daughter had been wondering if there was a way to get more tracks on a CD. Well, it was there all the time. The entire record collection of a small island on a single bit of plastic.

### Five Songs That Start With Someone Talking
*Leader of the Pack* (The Shangri-Las)
*My Boyfriend's Back* (The Angels)
*New Rose* (The Damned)
*Never Ever* (All Saints)
*You're The First, The Last, My Everything* (Barry White)

### Baker Street
As the 1980s rolled on I left the bank and went to live and work as part of the Lee Abbey Christian Community in North Devon. I was still buying Christian music, but whenever regular music entered my stratosphere it always grabbed my attention. My first Christmas at Lee Abbey a good friend brought his cassette player into the greenhouse (we were gardeners) where we were prepping festive decorations for the Christmas houseparty. The likes of Chicago, Billy Joel and Elton John crept back into my life as we whiled away many happy hours that day.

One night we went to the pub with a group and I couldn't help but notice when Bruce Springsteen came on the jukebox and lit the place up with *Dancing in the Dark*, and not long after Gerry Rafferty with the timeless *Baker Street*.

That last song always reminds me of a time when I got lost in Weston-super-Mare. It was not long after we'd moved there, and I'd gone into town with some friends, and then for some reason found myself wandering home alone. I'm to navigation what a shark is to unicycling. So I soon got lost. At some point I noticed a road called Baker Street and that put the song in my head. It also somehow pointed me in the right direction.

But that's why I recall the incident. Songs always fill my head. They are often my reference point in life. It's frequently the way I remember events and people and dates. In the movie *Fever Pitch*, Arsenal obsessed Paul is walking along with his girlfriend Sarah. When she asks him what he's thinking he mutters something about trying to remember which DH Lawrence book is the longest. But as the conversation continues it's clear he's making that up. 'I can't always say football, can I?' he confesses. Well, for me it would be pop music. And these days movies too. My head is often jammed with songs and cinematic tales. And nowadays they often merge with biblical stuff too. It's a glorious surround-sound, widescreen megamix.

**Five Elton John Favourites**
*Don't Go Breaking My Heart* (with Kiki Dee)
*I'm Still Standing*
*Cold Heart* (with Dua Lipa)
*I Guess That's Why They Call It The Blues*
*Part Time Love*

Just a by-the-by here, if you want to hear a song with a similar sound and yet very different tone to *Don't Go Breaking My Heart*, try *Dylan and Caitlin* by Manic Street Preachers. That song is an uncanny and deliberate throwback to the '70s classic.

### Record Machine

And a word here about the aforementioned jukeboxes. I put many a pound in those slots in my drinking days. The soundtrack as important as the beer. The process of selecting three singles and watching the chosen disc being nabbed and hoisted into position was wonderful to behold. Mp3s on your phone are one thing, and very useful too. But there's nothing like the sound of that coin dropping, followed by the metallic whirr and crick of the 7inch dropping into place. It's a long time since I put anything into a jukebox, and these days it's probably about tapping your credit card on a pad. I just hope that if it's a computer disguised as an old record machine, they have replicated that old whirr and crick noise. So pleasing.

### Five Songs That Mention Jukeboxes

*I Love Rock 'n' Roll* (Joan Jett)
*I Knew the Bride* (Dave Edmunds)
*Juke Box Jive* (The Rubettes)
*Roll Over Beethoven* (Chuck Berry)
*Jump* (Van Halen)

Some space for any thoughts, doodlings, scribblings, top fives, or musical memories of your own.

**Factoids**

I too often know unnecessary random chart facts as well. My poor family suffer them at meal times. A recent one for your delectation – in 1984 Wham's *Last Christmas* was kept off the Christmas number one by Band Aid's *Do They Know It's Christmas*? This Christmas just gone, 39 years later, *Last Christmas* was kept off the Christmas top spot again by – yes – Food Aid's version of *Do They Know It's Christmas*? If someone mentions a song or a group I most likely find a fact or statistic about it stealing into my brain.

Did you know The Who never had a number one single? Just five number two hits. Boney M went all the way to number one for five weeks with *Rivers of Babylon* in 1978, then they dropped down to number eighteen but went all the way back up to number two when folks started playing the B side, *Brown Girl in the Ring*. Which means enough people had not bought it the first time to send it back up to number two!

Even though Rod Stewart was at number one for four weeks in May 1977, with the double A-side single *First Cut is the Deepest* and *I Don't Wanna Talk About It*, and was in the top forty for twelve weeks, he did not make the year's top twenty bestselling singles. Why do I remember that? Why?? These pieces of musical litter continue to swish around the windmills of my mind.

I guess part of my obsession comes from keeping a record of the charts for five years ('76 to '81) and also from buying the *Guinness Book of British Hit Singles*. (As far as I was concerned that was the real *Guinness Book of Records*.) I loved gathering facts and information about and behind the songs and singers.

When, in Autumn 1976, I told my friend next door about my chart-keeping, I gave him my notebook so he could quiz me on it. He promptly asked me what was at number thirty on a recent week. I told him that was too obscure and unfair, and then remembered it was a band called Can with a song I had never heard called *I Want More*. More than 46 years ago and here it is, still in my head.

### Seven Days of the Week
*Manic Monday* (The Bangles)
*Ruby Tuesday* (The Rolling Stones)
*Wednesday Week* (The Undertones)
*Thursday* (Jess Glynn)
*Friday I'm in Love* (The Cure)
*Saturday Night* (Whigfield)
*Sunday Bloody Sunday* (U2)

### Seven Months of the Year
*January February* (Barbara Dixon – two for one there)
*April Skies* (The Jesus and Mary Chain)
*September* (Earth Wind and Fire)
*Goodbye October* (Adrian Snell)
*November Rain* (Guns 'n' Roses)
*December '63* (The Four Seasons)

### Guinness
*The Guinness Book of British Hit Singles* gave me access to so much random information. I thought David Essex

had only ever had three hits – two number ones in *Gonna Make You a Star* and *Hold Me Close,* and a lesser hit with a single we'd bought called *Cool Out Tonight*. But no! It seems he recorded loads of other things. I also discovered song titles that filled me with wonder and curiosity. *Ride a White Swan* by Marc Bolan. What did that sound like? And possibly *Starman* by Bowie too. I read these titles before hearing them.

It's hard to remember now all the songs I first saw in that book, before actually wrapping my ears around them. Nowadays when you read a title in a book or magazine you can go straight to YouTube. When I first read *31 Songs* by Nick Hornby I was grabbed by his passion for his favourite tunes. It was some years before I could actually find out what many of them sounded like. Now anything is out there, and YouTube has replaced sitting by your radio with a cassette recorder and a packet of Crawfords Cheddars.

It blew my mind for a while when I first discovered Spotify. What!? You mean I can listen to anything? Where do I start? All those albums I used to have, all those albums my friends had, all those albums people talked about and I never heard, not to mention all those albums in the charts right now... it went on and on.

The first song I ever downloaded was not actually for me. A friend at Lee Abbey (this was in our second stint working there in the noughties) needed a copy of *Achy Breaky Heart* by Billy Ray Cyrus. We were on dial up and it took an hour to come down the line. A three-minute song. My first 1GB memory stick cost me £129. Now you

131

can probably get 129GB for not much more than a quid. But I digress.

### ~~Five~~ Seven Hits That Started Life as B-sides

*King Fu Fighting* (Carl Douglas)
*The Model* (Kraftwerk)
*We Will Rock You* (Queen)
*How Soon is Now* (The Smiths)
*Green Onions* (Booker T. and the MGs)
*Maggie May* (Rod Stewart)
*Unchained Melody* (The Righteous Brothers)

### Timeline

I'm realising that this book is jumping all over the place events wise, so here's a quick synopsis of the overall story.

I was born in Stoke-on Trent 24th December 1962 (feel free to send presents and money). Moved to Cornwall in 1969. Went to Redruth Grammar School then Comprehensive School 1974 to 1977. Moved to Weston-super-Mare 1977. Went to Broadoak Comprehensive 1977 to 1979. Worked in NatWest bank 1979 to 1984. Moved to Lee Abbey 1984 to 1988. Worked in Christian drama and mime 1988 till 1997. In Insight Theatre Company from 1990 to 1992. Got married in 1994. Got a bit lost between 1997 and 2001. Returned to live and work at Lee Abbey as a family from 2002 to 2011. Started life again as a writer and speaker in 2011.

## Jazz and Plastic

So, back to Lee Abbey in the mid-'80s. More music from my past came looking for me, when I discovered that another gardening friend Rich shared my passion for 1970s music. We happily crooned our own versions of *Ca Plane Pour Moi* by Belgian punk Plastic Bertrand, and Joe Jackson's *Is She Really Going Out with Him?* as we watered strawberries and dug leeks.

Music was a shared language for us, and a means of great fun. We laughed long and hard at ourselves as we revisited and sent up various tunes. So many songs, so little work done. When Rich left Lee Abbey I dug out my old single of *Too Much Heaven* and got our other team mates to sign it for him.

Rich was also a great jazz pianist and he often used to improvise pieces adding his cool voiceover about us having appalling accidents as we cut the Lee Abbey lawns. I finally got to dress up as a punk at Lee Abbey, it took going to a Christian community to get me spiking my hair and putting on ripped t-shirts.

I finally got the chance to sing in a punk band too, as a group of us mocked up our own maverick rebels – The

Gatecrashers. I couldn't sing too well... which was perfect really.

In true punk style we sang our classic *I Really Hate Songs When You Can't Hear the Words*. It was only short and died abruptly at the end. But it was up there with *Pretty Vacant* and *London Calling*.

I've always been a performer one way or another, and dying my hair green and dabbing on black eyeliner released my inner Plastic Bertrand. A great time.
Years later when we visited Disneyland in Paris I had a go at being a kind of punk prophet too. A rebel with a cause. I spotted the statue of the mouse and the master, so I just had to kneel and

bow, as I felt we were all worshipping at the altar of Walt and Mickey.

Not sure anyone noticed, but then Ezekiel was told that no one would pay attention to him either. I submit the picture on the previous page as evidence, milord.

And as a tenuous link to my Lee Abbey gardening days...

**Plant-based Songs for this Eco Age**
*Rose Garden* (Lynn Anderson)
*Green Green Grass* (Tom Jones)
*Fields of Gold* (Sting)
*Flowers in the Rain* (The Move)
*Nutbush City Limits* (Ike and Tina Turner – Nutbush is in Tennessee, but probably has bushes or plants)
*I Talk to the Trees* (Clint Eastwood)
*Combine Harvester* (The Wurzels)

**Animals**
As my time at Lee Abbey drew to a close in the summer of 1988, another friend, Rob, performed a mime with one of the girls on community. It was about rejecting or helping each other, to the Ben E. King song *Stand By Me*, and I think it changed my life a bit. It was the first time I'd seen this kind of thing, a piece of drama with a message, drawing on a regular song. And so the principle lodged in my brain.

Over the next few years I began concocting various dramatic pieces to chart music, including nicking Rob's *Stand By Me* piece. In 1990 five of us ex-Lee Abbey friends set up a Christian theatre company, *Insight*, and we performed in schools a great deal, so using pop music seemed to be a great bridge into the kids' lives. We presented pieces to *Another Day in Paradise* by Phil Collins, Frankie Lymons' *Why Do Fools Fall in Love,* and Kate Bush's *Them Heavy People.* Along with others.

Even rave music proved useful as it provided an urgent, fast-paced instrumental soundtrack. I remember presenting the crucifixion to tracks by Undercover and The Prodigy. And then finishing with the resurrection to *Tubthumping*, with its refrain, 'I get knocked down, but I get up again...'

I started this book with a quote about sunshine from The Temptations' *My Girl*, we used to use that to gather a crowd when we were doing street theatre. Our *Insight* answerphone also drew on an old classic, The Animals' *House of the Rising Sun.* 'There is a house in Booker Lane, but nobody's at home. Just leave your name and number here, and speak right after the tone.'

At a party back in the '70s I had been grabbed by another Animals' number, *Don't Let Me Be Misunderstood,* though I had not known it was The Animals singing it. *We Gotta Get Out of This Place* was another of theirs, a song given extra meaning for the soldiers in the Vietnam War. It's the sort of tune that gets in my head and I'll probably be singing it all morning after typing this.

### Christians

I had also begun to buy regular music again. And it began with a band called The Christians. (I had allowed

136

myself to buy Mr Mister's album *Welcome to the Real World* in the mid-eighties as it contained their great track *Kyrie*, and 'Kyrie Eleison' means 'Lord, have mercy'.)

If any secular band was going to sound as if they might be Christians then surely it was The Christians. They even had a track on their album called *Born Again*. I never found out what faith they had. But I bought their album, and that cassette was jammed with catchy thought-provoking numbers.

It was the start of a new era when I began buying albums again. Fleetwood Mac's *Tango In the Night* was popular and for me an easy choice. I found myself slipping easily back into that world, but I was different now. Music didn't seem to have the same hold over me, and I was thinking about ways I could use it. Inspired by Rob's *Stand By Me*.

These days I sometimes get inspiration from the themes of contemporary songs. A few years back I was driving to a meeting when Jess Glynne's *Thursday* came on the radio, with its lyrics about not covering up. It nestled in my head and set me thinking, and so I wrote the following.

**From the Heart**
Thank you that we can worship you
as we are,
no need for pretence,
don't have to be good or look good,
or have all the answers.
no need to cover up,
or say the right words,

or hide from ourselves and you.
Don't need to use the right words,
or know the right songs,
or even sing in tune.
Thank you that we can come to you
as we are,
any time of the day or night,
any place in the world,
any time of life.
Being honest and genuine,
offloading our fears and troubles,
because you understand,
and you care.

I realise now more than ever how spiritual music is, all kinds of music, in all kinds of ways. And songs so often give voice to our longings, hopes, dreams and secret prayers. From a very early age children sing, I love hearing Lucy singing to herself as she goes about her day. It rises from within us, whether we are tuneful or not, and if you want examples of honest songs, just take a gander through the psalms. Pain, pleasure, faith, doubt, wondering, memories, visions, sadness, questions, certainty and sorrow are all writ large there.

The Christians may or may not have considered themselves a spiritual band, but in a song like *Ideal World* they expressed the psalmists' longings for a better world full of freedom and justice. A world where all is put right once more. A Revelation 21 kind of world. And an Isaiah 65 (verses 17-25) kind of world.

**Scatterlings**

In 1989 I had the chance to visit friends in South Africa and while there I had two musical highlights. In Durban a group of us went to see Johnny Clegg and Savuka, a vibrant evening of Zulu-infused rock, complete with vigorous, exuberant cultural dancing. It was an engrossing, unforgettable evening. Their song *Scatterlings of Africa* featured in the film *Rainman* and you can find it on YouTube.

I then travelled down what is known as The Garden Route to the Cape stopping off on the way to see my old mate Rich from those gardening, singing and laughter days at Lee Abbey. He was by then a curate in Port Elizabeth. We spent a few mad days reminiscing and reliving the good times.

In Cape Town I stayed with a friend who took me to The Brass Bell pub where we sat on a sea wall to watch the band Bright Blue perform under a sun-splashed South African sky. You can find several of their songs on YouTube including the moving *Weeping*.

I also had a chance to see some Zulu theatre, performed by The Loft Theatre Company. I didn't understand a word, it wasn't in English, and yet was completely absorbed by the power and presence of the physical performance.

Afterwards I wrote several lively physical theatre pieces which we went on to perform in *Insight Theatre Company*. I also bought albums by both bands before I headed home. This is why art is so important, stories and songs and pictures can connect us in a way that dialogue can sometimes set us apart. Behind everything we say there is at least five other things unsaid. (That's a Hopwood fact, not a scientific one.) Plus there can be a lot of emotional static in the air.

So though we may not communicate clearly with the words we say, with songs and stories that's an advantage. We can place ourselves in the gaps in those sketches, and that music, and those recited tales, connect our stories with those being told and sung. *Stay Free* is such a special song for me, not because it tells my story, far from it, but it has enough about it that enables me to hang my story on it and find myself in it.

### Commitments

In 1990 Alan Parker's film *The Commitments* won the Bafta for best film of the year. In *Insight* we had been hoping to see it for a while and as result of the award it came back to our local cinema for a late night showing, so we tripped down the Wycombe Six. What a movie. Jampacked with great performances, searing dialogue, vibrant characters, and gripping soul songs. The likes of *Try a Little Tenderness*, *Dark End of the Street,* and *Mustang Sally* burned themselves into my being and wouldn't go away.

I felt good for a week afterwards and bought not one soundtrack album but volume two as well. For a long time I named it as my favourite movie of all time. Even though the thing was littered with arguments and bantering and falling out, there was something about it which made me feel so alive. A group of Dublin misfits following their dreams. As it said on the poster – 'They

140

had absolutely nothing, but they were willing to risk it all.'

Makes me think of those first disciples, Andrew, James, Mary, Martha, Peter, Salome, Joanna, Bartholomew, Thomas, Susanna... a group of folks who were not power players or rich kids. But in Jesus they found someone worth everything. Worth the dream, the risk, the following, the letting go. They didn't quite have absolutely nothing, but they were drawn to the one who asked the question, 'What do you gain if you win the world, and in doing so lose your soul?' They found their answer in him.

And that takes me back to a conversation I had sometime around 1985, when a friend and I mused about Abraham walking into the unknown, and what that might have been like, and even now as I recall that there's a feeling that stirs in that distant memory. We all have our unknowns, and the invisible God calling us to follow. Sometimes we do, sometimes we don't. But the call goes on. A voice on the wind, a whisper amongst the clatter and distractions.

Abraham was given a sign, one he would see night after night after night. The stars. 'Look up Abraham and count them.' Every evening he would see that promise writ large, the promise of a future and a hope. When we moved here to this house I found that above our bed, on the ceiling over the place where a cot used to be, there are glow-in-the-dark stars. Every night I can look up and think of Abraham. And the God we share. The God who calls us on. The God who is with us. Emmanuel.

### Number One

As I began to get back into pop music I was reminded of something. Popular music changes. The decline of punk and new wave had been shock enough, but now dance music was starting to dominate. S-Express had a huge pulse-driven hit in 1988, and by the time the '90s came around the top ten was starting to fill up with word-free dance tracks. Great for boogieing and shimmying, although nobody boogied and shimmied in the '90s of course, but terrible on the radio. Where were the proper songs? The ballads? The anthems? The protest cries?

I was pleasantly shocked one day when I walked into WH Smiths and the chart listing (Smiths used to sell singles and display the top forty) showed The Clash at number one. What!? The Clash? *My* Clash? Number one in 1991? What was happening? Turns out Levi's was happening. They were littering their adverts with classic songs. The previous year the jeans people had stormed the charts with Steve Miller's early '70s number *The Joker*, and now they had dug out *Should I Stay or Should I Go* from 1982, and were bombarding the hip '90s kids with it. Result!

Like The Jam before them the punk boys had crept into pop stardom. It guaranteed that, along with *London Calling,* 'the only band that mattered' would be remembered by the General Public for two songs at least.

It probably sounds odd to say, but I found the change in chart music disorientating. I was still only in my late twenties but already I was feeling out of touch. And annoyed by not being able to control things. Rap was becoming ever more popular. It had been fun when *Oops Upside Your Head* had us diving on the dancefloor to do the rowing moves, but now it was getting everywhere. Talking Talking Talking. I know I'm being unfair, and really just showing my Victor Meldrew side, but for a while it seemed as if the hip hop folks were taking all the great tracks from the '70s, mangling them, sampling them, and talking over the great tunes. And I wish I had a fiver for every time a song had the line 'Put your hands in the air like you just don't…' I'd have ooh £37.50. or something like that.

I doth protest too much methinks… because whatever I say, it's part of the creativity that is stitched into this world. Life changes, it moves on, art develops. Lots of things develop. And I may not like it, but I can't stop it.

King Canute went down to the water and commanded the waves to stop shuffling, not because he thought he could, but to prove he couldn't. Creation won't stand still. So apologies again if hip hop is your bag, why shouldn't it be? When Elvis pitched up some people were afraid, very afraid. Same with The Beatles and The Stones.

And then The Sex Pistols and The Clash put the heebie-jeebies up a generation. So I'm in good company. Like Canute and the water, I can't stop the progress, the movement of the tide. The musical waves keep coming, and all of that said, there were still plenty of great songs around in those early '90s. Great bands and singers still appeared on Top of the Pops. Showaddywaddy, Darts and Matchbox may have been long gone, but all was not lost. And then, in 1993, the sun rose once more. It had been creeping up on us for a while...

### Great Things

Nowadays the bands of the mid-'90s seem to shy away from the Britpop tag. They just want to be rock bands. And I understand that. However, it was a joyous period for me, when so many guitar bands came through, reminiscent of those New Wave days. And the label Britpop gave it a focus and a rallying cry. Whether or not we call it Britpop, it was a flurry of creativity and colour. Pulp and Blur and Oasis and Ocean Colour Scene and Echobelly... they filled the airwaves and gave our kitchen in Woking a much-needed music-lift. The charts were interesting again! I was working with another mime artist and good friend Ken at the time, and we performed pieces about friendship to *Wonderwall* and about Creation to Echobelly's *Great Things*. We may have used other Britpop tracks in our work.

I loved that period. Lynn and I got married in 1994 and that's when the airwaves exploded with the new sounds. *TFI Friday* was on channel 4 and Chris Evans was in his element. His improvised approach and glut of ideas was inspiring. I pinched his fast-paced either/or interview style. Do you like tea or coffee? Are you a morning person or an evening person? Is the glass half full or half empty? That sort of thing. Great for warming up an audience.

Certain presenters, writers and artists inspire me to do more. To go further. To keep creating and pushing boundaries. What's the next unexpected thing I could use to communicate the Bible? What's the thing no one has yet thought about that could be useful? How can I do things that help people connect with God, not just offering a talk, but an experience? This is what the prophets were about, smashing jars, building boats, buying fields, howling wildly, head-shaving, and going au naturelle. Nothing was too far for them. Nothing too extreme if it helped people stop and tune into God.

In his book *Everything is Spiritual*, Rob Bell describes preaching as being part performance art, part poetry, part guerrilla theatre, part recovery meeting, part subversive rhetoric. I like that description, not least the recovery meeting bit, part of what any Christian teacher is doing is letting God's light shine out through the cracks in their own life.

It's the biggest challenge to communicate with integrity. And if St Paul is right then we're all just pots full of cracks letting God's light do the work. Or as someone else once said, one beggar telling another where to find food.

The guerrilla theatre idea is fascinating too. I can tell you about the prodigal, but what trail can I lay so that you come with me as I follow it home? In the early days of Hollywood film makers used to have a wildy on set, a person who could come up with the next mad idea when the film makers weren't sure what to do next. The prophets were wildys. Unafraid to go with the divine nudges for the sake of rescuing people. For the sake of laying that trail of grace which leads the prodigals home.

**A Britpop Era Top ~~Five~~ Ten**

*The Day We Caught the Train* (Ocean Colour Scene)

*Common People* (Pulp)

*Disco 2000* (Pulp)

*Great Things* (Echobelly)

*Alright* (Supergrass)

*Don't Look Back in Anger* (Oasis)

*Stand by Me* (Oasis)

*Good Enough* (Dodgy)

*Buddy Holly* (Weezer)

*Linger* (The Cranberries)

Some space for any thoughts, doodlings, scribblings, top fives, or musical memories of your own.

### Honey

My favourite band of the '90s however, did not emerge from that period. Back in the 1980s the Housemartins sang about *Happy Hour* and *Caravan of Love*. That latter song was almost a Christmas number one, and it featured an unexpected gospel tune *When I First Met Jesus* on the B-side. I was given their album *London 0 Hull 4* at Christmas 1986.

I lost track of them over the next couple of years, till a friend played me a song in 1990 by a new band called The Beautiful South. I instantly fell in love with the infectious melody and smooth sound. Turned out The Housemartins had disbanded and morphed into this new group. All except one Norman Cook, who had left and morphed into Fatboy Slim.

I bought everything by them over the next decade, I particularly loved the searing lyrics set to the sweetest of tunes. Paul Heaton, the song writer, used to go away to a dreary place to pen the words, then he'd head off to somewhere sunny to write the tunes. A brilliant idea.

GK Chesterton once said, 'More flies are caught with honey than with vinegar.' Truth doesn't need to be delivered with a straight face. It can be entertaining, memorable, uplifting. Even hard truth. Jesus knew that. Paul Heaton's happy tunes came with a punch. Made you smile and elbowed you in the ribs at the same time. Put a spring in your step and pulled the rug. I loved that.

### Gotta Get a Message to You

U2's Bono once said something like, 'Have the peace that passes understanding, but don't be at peace with the world, because the world is not at peace.' History is littered with musical cries about a world gone bad. The biblical book of psalms is full of such tunes. And they don't always make for easy reading. The cries for a better life are scrawled across this book which sits smack in the centre of your Bible.

In 1992 Arrested Development released *Mr Wendal* another hip hop track that grabbed me. (I'm starting to realise I like more than I thought.) It was all about a homeless guy who had nothing and yet reflected back to the rest of us what was important in life. It's catchy and pleasing on the ear, yet at the same time comes with bite. One of those great message songs.

Phil Collins wrote *Another Day in Paradise*, this one about a homeless girl, and a call to appreciate how much you and I have. Two years later Kirsty MacColl sang about poverty, wealth and injustice in *Walking Down Madison*.

Black Eyed Peas gave us *Where's the Love*, in which they looked around at the world and the way we destroy one another, and offered us that question. 'What's wrong with the world?' was the opening line, which puts me in mind of that famous response – 'I am.' I'm wrong with the world, I'm at odds. I can't point the finger and hurl scorn and accusations when in doing that very pointing I'm only adding to the Everest of blame and criticism and prejudice which fuels the anger and resentment and hard-hearted nature of things.

Author Chimamanda Ngozi Adichie gave one of the Reith lectures last year, on freedom of speech, and when a comment was raised by one of the audience members, about the right to criticise others on social media being technically illegal these days, she responded along the lines of, 'Don't do it then, do something else, do something better.'

And that brings me back to a thought from Bono, and his call for lives of inspiration rather than mere preaching at people. Not easy of course, very, very hard in fact. I'd rather just pour out my opinions than my time and energy and compassion. But it's a target we can aim for, with the help of God's spirit, a light to sail towards, in a world where casting darkness can be popular. Better to light a candle than waste energy on throwing curses at the murk, as someone once said.

And that brings us to Matthew chapter 5, and what we call The Beatitudes. Jesus's call to be merciful peacemakers, with hearts set on a better, kinder world.

And *that* brings us to The Isley Brothers and their song *Harvest for the World*, later covered by The Christians. A call for everyone to have enough, a hunger for justice rather than a hunger for food. Bob and Midge and a gang of bleary-eyed eighties stars dragged themselves out of bed, make-up barely applied, to record *Feed the World*.

And after four Christmas number ones raising money for The Trussell Trust food charity, Ladbaby had a record-setting fifth Christmas number one with his own version of *Feed the World – Feed the UK*. With every copy bought we were helping to do just that.

*Saviour's Day* was a different kind of message song. Another Christmas number one but a reminder of whose birthday we were celebrating. A call from our Creator to each of us on that Saviour's Day.

Cliff is famous for having lots of Christmas hits, but in truth he didn't have a proper Christmas-themed number one till 1988's *Mistletoe and Wine*, and *Saviour's Day* was only his second.

And the list of protest tunes goes on. Tracy Chapman's *Talking 'Bout a Revolution* (a call for equality and recognition for the working class), U2's *Sunday Bloody Sunday* (fourteen shot dead and fourteen injured in a peaceful protest in Derry), Billy Bragg's *Between the Wars* (a miner's cry for justice), The Clash's *Career Opportunities* (a plea for meaningful jobs) and their *Washington Bullets* (an anti-war song).

And of course The Wurzels' *Combine Harvester* was a crucial tune about... trying to woo a woman with heavy machinery. Maybe not that one then.

**Top Five Favourite Protest Songs**
*Talking 'Bout a Revolution* (Tracey Chapman)
*Good People Go* (Jack Johnson)
*Washington Bullets* (The Clash)
*Young, Gifted and Black* (Bob Andy and Marcia Griffiths)
*I Don't Like Mondays* (The Boomtown Rats)

**Retro**
In the late 1990s I started working part-time in the Victoria Theatre in Woking, we were struggling and needing more income. While I was there I met Alvin Stardust one night. He'd come to see a show and I was

selling programmes, and was a little starstruck. But I told him we had a mutual friend, a Christian singer Steve Flashman. I believe Alvin became a Christian in his later years.

He'd had hits during the glam period of the early 1970s with *My Coo Ca Choo, Jealous Mind, Red Dress* and *You, You, You*. I loved his look back then with that single black glove he wore. I once heard him speaking in a documentary about the '70s, and he said when *Jealous Mind* went to number one he was all alone in his hotel room, with no one to celebrate the achievement. I think he had been told he had to stay in there between performing, in order to protect his black-gloved mystique.

He came to the theatre on another occasion as part of a '70s retro show, with Suzie Quatro, and The Rubettes. The Rubettes brought the house down with their 1974 number one *Sugar Baby Love* (a hit originally offered to Showaddywaddy), but the highlight of the evening for me was Suzie Quatro singing *If You Can't Give Me Love*. One of those singles I played to death in 1978.

I also saw The Hollies do a gig in that theatre. And Roy Wood. That was a treat, I'd always loved his wall of sound, and *See My Baby Jive* had been on *Ten Years of Hits on Radio One*. Plus there was his festive glam track *I Wish It Could Be Christmas Every Day*.

It was Phil Spector who first came up with the wall of sound in the '60s and I had his Christmas collection. Brian Wilson of the Beach Boys wrote *God Only Knows* for Mr Spector after hearing *Will You Love Me Tomorrow* on the radio. He was driving and had to pull over to listen to the thing properly, he was so stunned by it. But Mr Spector turned Brian's song down, and so the Beach Boys went down in history with it instead.

I mentioned earlier that I'd never been a great concertgoer, so those Woking gigs were a bonus. I did see Cliff in the '80s at a Christmas gig in Bristol. And Rick Wakeman in Barnstaple. I also saw Marcel Marceau in London but as he was a mime artist that doesn't count. If he did sing it was silently. He did do a brilliant tight rope walking routine though. And a piece about wearing masks, a mime I subsequently pinched.

A man finds a bag of masks, and after trying on a few gets stuck with the smile on his face. He can't take it off and begins to sob. Still smiling. The real person is now hidden. Just as if he'd put on a fig leaf to hide his naked form. Powerful. I get so weary of the masks sometime. Yet still make trips to that bag and then find myself trapped behind the wrong face.

### ~~Five~~ Eight Glam Rock Favourites
*Virginia Plain* (Roxy Music)
*Good Love Can Never Die* (Alvin Stardust)
*This Town Ain't Big Enough for the Both of Us* (Sparks)
*Blockbuster* (The Sweet)
*Ride a White Swan* (T Rex)
*I Love to Boogie* (T Rex)
*Rebel Rebel* (David Bowie)
*See My Baby Jive* (Wizzard)

Typing that Alvin Stardust song makes me feel just a tad queasy. Which sounds odd, but then I do remember being sick at one point, after eating my favourite meal of baked beans on toast, and it put me off beans for quite a while. So perhaps *Good Love Can Never Die* was in the charts at the time. Interesting the way music can take you back like that.

### Kibera

As the new millennium kicked in and it turned out the world wasn't going to end, I had the incredible privilege of visiting Nairobi with a group of friends and a schools group from Worthing. The youngsters were studying Kibera in their course and so were having the chance to put feet on the ground and meet the people they were reading about. Kibera is just outside Nairobi and one of the biggest slums in the world.

I recall two musical moments from that time. One of the boys was clearly a Backstreet Boys fan, because from time to time he would break into a rendition of one of their songs *As Long As You Love Me*. I didn't know the song at the time, but his rendition was classy and confident, and I listened in and admired it quietly from afar, and then looked it up when I got home.

The other memory is a little more profound. The group leader, Steve, had warned us that conditions in Kibera might upset us, but as we walked through those pathways and were thronged by happy children who wanted to welcome us, there seemed no reason to be concerned about anything being too much.

Then we walked into the little church, and the women of Kibera were singing beautiful Kenyan worship songs. Oh my goodness. I was overwhelmed and could feel myself welling up. It was all I could do to keep myself together. The singing, the atmosphere, the presence of God... I will never forget it. It was beautiful. An extraordinary gift that day. It moves me now as I type this.

### Reasons

In the noughties we returned to work and live at Lee Abbey for nine years. I was frustrated about many things by that time, a bit of an emotional wreck as I approached my forties. I used to get quite frustrated about church services and would sometimes come out, slip home to our house on the Lee Abbey estate and put on some Ian Dury. Specifically *Reasons to Be Cheerful, Pt. 3*. His list of random, happy things lifted my spirits: 'Summer, Buddy Holly... being rather silly and porridge oats... the juice of a carrot, the smile of a parrot... health service glasses... cheddar cheese and pickle...'

I've just cherry-picked a few there, silly, wonderful, daft things about life. The tune was of course uplifting, and the sax solo in the middle is sublime and a little bit like something from Acker Bilk. There were times when I needed this daft and enriching shot in the arm.

I've sometimes found the predictability of church a tad wearisome, and have occasionally wondered if Jesus walked into a service whether he might stop, look around and say, 'A bit tidy in here, isn't it? Shall we bring a little of the unexpected?' (As long as I'm not speaking of course, otherwise it might disrupt my carefully crafted material. 😊)

Jesus's whole ministry seems to have been based on the unpredictable, the complications and interruptions. He did go along to organised Synagogue meetings, but sometimes caused a bit of a ruckus there. So much so that on one occasion they tried to shove him off a cliff. So much for 'Go in peace etc...'

I understand that many people need church to be safe and sure and reliable, especially in a rapidly changing world. And I'm happy to go along to services which are havens of calm and order. Places of refreshing, still waters and green pastures. But I just wonder how we might best communicate the Living Word. (I started this subject back on page 106 by the way. Thinking about new wineskins, and new mindsets.)

How can we give folk things they can take away which will help them through the week? Gifts from the God who is the pillar of cloud and fire, with us wherever we go, alive and present and active. Intensely interested in the highs and lows of our days and nights.

The God who spray-painted the galaxies with stars and planets and yet knows every human heart. And every song we sing. And if that turns out to be untidy, well, that's okay. The aim is not to have things watertight, not if we are looking to have hearts of flesh, receptive to a brand new divine and windswept spirit.

In his book *Surrender*, U2's Bono writes about the contradictions, and living with them, and surely going to church is a contradiction. We turn up with our heads full of last week's woes and worries and find ourselves singing about peace and faith. And that brings us back again to the profound truth in Leonard Cohen's song

*Anthem*, and the light that comes in through the cracks in our lives. We are cracked. Our churches are cracked. Our streets are cracked. We don't have a perfect offering, we only have our ragged selves. And the paradox is that this is enough, and it is not enough.

We come to the God who loves us so much he welcomes us open-armed, just as we are, but loves us too much to leave us that way. And so the wrestling begins, and we carry the contradictions of believing in a God of love, and yet are often judging and rejecting others. We trust in a God of peace, and yet often feel torn apart. And we hold onto a God of hope, and yet we're often caught in drifts of despair.

And so we look to a cross, and find the son of man embracing the contradictions, changing the world not in some glorious superhero kind of way, but in a broken and diminished state. Looking like he's lost every fight, and the entire war. And only in swallowing that emptiness can he bring fullness of life. Only in drinking that cup of squalor and anguish and hatred and decay can he draw beauty and creativity and wonder and kindness from us.

He dies and we are reborn. He rises and we are still coming to terms with it. Resurrection is not easy to live with or express in a world which is small and preoccupied with meagre distractions. The name Israel means 'one who wrestles with God', and here we are in that very place ourselves. One minute sitting at peace with God, the next minute disappointed with ourselves. And then back to peace with God, and then back to discomfort with ourselves. On and on.

157

Gosh, that was a tangent, back to the music.

Some space for any thoughts, doodlings, scribblings, top fives, or musical memories of your own.

### Moved

Ian Durie's *Hit Me With Your Rhythm Stick* is also a great feelgood number. Warren Huart presents videos on YouTube about the making of classic songs (look up his channel Produce Like a Pro) and when he talked about *Rhythm Stick* I was moved to see he had a moment when he choked up. I love that. He was so moved by the track and the story that went with it that he couldn't hold in his feelings.

I do think that when we are moved by good things in this life it's often a sign of God with us, peeping out at us, showing us his glory in those things which make life better rather than worse, those things which lift our spirits.

### Jump!

When our first daughter Amy was very little, we used to play a collection of '70s and '80s songs in the car (now there's a surprise). One of them was Stacy Lattisaw's *Jump to the Beat* a disco number from 1980. In the chorus the line invites us to get with the beat and jump, and the backing singers then repeat the word 'Jump'.

As we were sitting in the car one day with Amy we became aware that she was joining in with every 'Jump!' perfectly on time. You remember these things,

I'll never forget the day I was walking through our doctor's surgery car park with our younger daughter, Lucy, and out of nowhere she suddenly said, 'Paintballing.' I doubted that we would have taught her that word, she was only two. Then I spotted a van with the word etched in a flourish across the side. Lucy had read it. And I was knocked sideways just a little. She has always been very good at reading. She was able to read the messages in her cards on her third birthday.

Amy's been a singer ever since that Jump! incident. When she was a bit older, about five or six, we filmed her standing on a chair in our kitchen singing The Sugababes song *About You Know*. It was on YouTube for a while but not anymore, I think I took it down. These days she likes nothing more than putting on music in the kitchen while she's cooking a meal for us.

Lucy sings too while she's doing all kinds of things. Often it's just there and I don't notice it, but at moments when I do it always warms my heart a little.

So I wonder, did the heavenly father come running the first time his young son sang a song? And did he stop everything to hear the first words he uttered, and to see the first bumbling steps he took? Did he reach down a little as if he might save his son from tottering over? And did he beckon to the angels with cries of, 'Look, look, look!' Did he draw near at night while Jesus slept and brush stray hair from his son's forehead? And did he hear our first song, our first words, and watch our first steps, and beckon to the angels, with the cry, 'Look, look, look!'

### Strong

One of my favourite Robbie Williams songs is *Strong*. He sings about the way others might look at him and think he's strong, but they're not right. There's an odd paradox in standing up in front of others and telling them about your faith. It's a privilege too. But you can talk for ten minutes about your weaknesses and struggles, and yet come across as strong and sorted out.

By virtue of being able to stand in front of others and speak up (one of the top three fears apparently) it looks as if whatever you say you are powerful. And that's why I love Robbie Williams's song. Because I'm not strong.

We speakers also must wrestle constantly with the temptation to tell people what to do... i.e. to do things we don't do ourselves. It's tempting to say all the right things, when sometimes people need to hear the troublesome things, the weak things, the mistakes and foibles.

Robbie Williams has been through the mill, like so many stars. Fame is bad for you. I'm sure of that. I recently saw the Whitney Houston biopic *I Wanna Dance with Somebody*. She was an incredibly gifted person ravaged by the savage baggage that comes with fame. And then there's Michael Jackson, and Amy Winehouse, and Prince and Mamma Cass. They may well have wanted to be famous of course, but we all want stuff that's not good for us.

The snag with pop music is it creates pop stars. And those of us who dwell in that collective known as the General Public do not deal well with anyone who looks like they might have more ability than we do. We make them heroes and wonder-people and gods. Because we were made to worship. And we can't help it.

Worship is about where you place your energy, money, time and resources. It's not merely about singing songs, though we often worship people who are singing songs. But those people are not strong. No matter how perfectly they are presented to us.

There's a fascinating passage in the book of Isaiah in the Bible. It's in Chapter 44 and reads like this – 'How foolish are those who manufacture idols to be their gods. These highly valued objects are really worthless. They themselves are witnesses that this is so, for their idols neither see nor know. No wonder those who worship them are put to shame. Who but a fool would make his own god – an idol that cannot help him one bit!'

This refers to idols made of wood and metal and stone, but it's close enough to those idols made of flesh and blood. They cannot help us. Not in the way we want, they cannot fill the gap inside. Rock'n'roll won't fill my soul. And yet the paradox goes on.

Robbie told us we were wrong, and we still worshipped him with our time and energy and money. We wanted him to sing that, because we could relate to it, even if perhaps we didn't really quite believe him. He looked and sounded too cool, too professional, to be weak in any way. Bruce Springsteen's latest album is called *Only The Strong Survive*, but that's not really the case. No one survives, not forever. Not without the rescuing hand of the one who made himself weak for us.

### Hoovered My Head

In the early noughties I came across a worship album with a difference. In 1994 Fat and Frantic brought a doo wop worship collection called *Precious Lord*, it was

163

actually credited to Fat and Frantic & Friends, and one of my mates from Lee Abbey in 1984 featured on it, Chris who had brought his cassette player into the greenhouse as we prepped the Christmas decorations.

Chris and I had ripped off many songs in our eighteen months together on that community. We modelled ourselves a little on The Two Ronnies, turning old favourites into comedy numbers. A particular highlight was rehashing *Summer Nights* and *You're The One That I Want* from *Grease*, turning them into pot plant selling songs. 'I got plants, they're multiplying, and we're losing control...'

Fat and Frantic never seemed to take themselves too seriously, with previous albums entitled *Aggressive Sunbathing* and *Waxing a Hottie*. One memorable single was called *Last Night My Wife Hoovered My Head*. So *Precious Lord* was full of great worship songs, but done in a different way, and a real favourite was the kids' chorus *Be Bold, Be Strong*. You can find it on YouTube if you look for a Fat and Frantic playlist.

We used the song in various ways whilst at Lee Abbey, including doing a dance routine about rival gangs in one of the summer shows. I once had the chance to play Rummikub with Fat and Frantic's drummer and his son when we crossed paths at a Christian Festival one year. I might have even won.

**Five Bird Songs (I warned you about this on page 8)**
*Albatross* (Fleetwood Mac)
*Songbird* (Fleetwood Mac)
*Blackbird* (The Beatles)

*Wings of a Dove* (Madness)
*Rockin' Robin* (Michael Jackson)


**Common**

In 2007 a song called *She's So Lovely* began racing across the airwaves. It was by a band called Scouting for Girls At the time it stuck in my mind because something about it reminded me of *Back of my Hand* by the Jags. I downloaded it and put it on in the car. (I'd have walked into a record store, proffered cash and walked out again with a solid bit of vinyl under my arm in those heady *Back of My Hand* days.)

Before long not only was my wife a fan of those Scouting chaps, but also our older daughter too. We loved the witty, wry lyrics, and the short sharp tunes. I have a memory of us racing round the house to *She's So Lovely* but I may be imagining that.

Our older daughter and I have continued to be fans, listening to pretty much everything they've done since. Amy even tracks down their obscure singles and B-sides. That's what makes them unique for me, as a family we all loved that first album, and now Amy and I continue to have their music in common.

There's nothing quite like that moment of discovery when you meet someone, think you have nothing in common, and then discover they bought the same album, or recorded the same songs.


**Battering Ram**

Amy and I also share a love for the songs of Meat Loaf and Jim Steinman. I first bought *Bat Out of Hell* back in my banking days. Meat and Jim couldn't get a record company to take it when they trawled it round the big boys. Nobody understood this Wagnerian storytelling rock, especially as punk had just rewritten the rule book and demanded everything be done and dusted in two minutes fifty-nine seconds. The album version of the title track is close to ten minutes long, there was only room for seven tracks on the disc. But producer Todd Rundgren saw something in it and put it out for the rest of us to hear.

It was a slow burner but has gone on to be one of the biggest selling albums of all time. I love the sound and melodies and the drama of it, but mostly I love Steinman's lyrics. He manages to say so much in a sentence using phrases like a gun in the eye, and riding like a battering ram. Taking the words from someone's mouth while kissing them. In the words of my daughter Amy, 'It's as if he writes poetry and disguises it as a rock song.'

There's not a lyrical cliché in sight. Every phrase smacks of original ideas and images. So poetic and visceral. And to such great tunes. Listening always makes me think I should work a bit harder at my writing. (Reading this book you might think that too.)

The singles from *Bat Out of Hell* were relatively minor hits, the title track only made number fifteen in the UK. But fifteen years later, after many albums and adventures, Jim and Meat were back with the sequel, which put them squarely at number one in both the singles and album charts.

And talking of originality I've often thought that Abba manage to avoid many clichés too. Perhaps writing in their second language somehow gives them an advantage there. Have a read of some of their lyrics sometime and you'll see what I mean. They also put their real-life troubles on vinyl with the likes of *The Winner Takes It All* and *One of Us.*

**Top ~~Five~~ Six Meat Loaf/Jim Steinman Favourites**
*Rock and Roll Dreams Come Through*
*Bat Out of Hell*
*You Took the Words Right Out of My Mouth*
*Dead Ringer*
*I'd Do Anything for Love*
*Total Eclipse of the Heart* (by Bonnie Tyler)

**Safari**
My safari with pop music has continued, though I'm too old for Radio One these days. I've been too old for a good while now, and I'm heading for too old for Radio Two as well, now that all the DJs are changing again. I do get a sense of despondency about losing touch and missing out. And streaming has affected things, it has made everything available, but that doesn't mean we appreciate it all. Or even know it's there.

I love the internet for its many opportunities, but there is no doubt we have created a monster that sometimes appears to be devouring us, one byte at a time. When I went to see the movie *Bohemian Rhapsody* with Amy, as I came out I wondered if I still had some of Queen's music somewhere. I discovered I had lots of it.

But that's the thing, back in those vinyl days I'd have known immediately which Queen albums I had in my collection. Now they get buried somewhere amongst the thousands of photos and millions of word documents. The brilliant *Somebody to Love* is just another file in a folder in a folder in a folder.

### Yesterday and That Thing

And talking of music in films, I love Danny Boyle and Richard Curtis's *Yesterday* – with the fantastic premise of a world where no one has ever heard of The Beatles, except for a struggling young singer-songwriter who can't get a break. Overnight Jack discovers that he has all these great songs at his fingertips, and no one realises The Beatles made them up. What would you do? For a while at least Jack wows the world with his extraordinary back catalogue. Fabulous. And then there is the wonderful *That Thing You Do*. Directed by Tom Hanks and set in the '50s, The Wonders are an upcoming band who record a feelgood single and take it on the road. The moment when they first hear it played on the radio is one of the best joyous moments, as one by one the members of the band discover the truth, and end up dancing together in the local washing machine store.

### Favourite Beatles Songs (It's about time really)

*I Wanna Hold Your Hand*
*I Saw Her Standing There*

*Come Together*
*Let It Be*
*With A Little Help From My Friends*
*Twist and Shout*
*Penny Lane*
*Do You Want to Know A Secret*
*From Me to You*
*Here Comes the Sun*

It's hard to imagine now the impact of these songs when people first heard them. To me they were just pop songs on the radio. Craig Brown writes about this in his book *One Two Three Four: The Beatles in Time*. A young teenager was sitting in his mother's car in New Jersey when a certain song came on the radio. It affected his whole demeanour, a strange sensation gripped his body, and it seemed as if the radio was glowing as it fought to contain this incredible sound. In the coming summer he worked to earn enough to buy a guitar, and his life was set on a whole new course. The song? *I Wanna Hold Your Hand*, and that fourteen-year-old was a youngster called Bruce Springsteen.

Some space for any thoughts, doodlings, scribblings, top fives, or musical memories of your own.

## So Many Songs

In the noughties I got hooked on The Killers (bought their first three albums), also Razorlight, Noah and the Whale, and The Fratellis. I loved The Fratellis' first album *Costello Music*, the very name seemed to hark back to Elvis and those New Wave days. The sound was stompy and shouty and catchy. A little bit Slade perhaps, a little bit Libertines. *Chelsea Dagger* had folks leaping around again.

Razorlight's *America* was a perfectly formed radio song. (In my 'umble 'pinion.) It seemed for a time that there was a resurgence of good bands. I don't of course comment in any way as an expert here, or anywhere else in the book. There were plenty of other bands around, The Editors, Switchfoot, Franz Ferdinand... so I'm only mentioning the bands that caught my attention.

Later The Vaccines came along, hailed as the saviours of rock'n'roll. They were edgy and fast and a little bit furious. They've calmed down now but still make very listenable music. There may well have been loads more bands, but I was getting out of touch. And listening to lots of old music.

In his book *31 Songs* Nick Hornby cites Bruce Springsteen's *Thunder Road* as the song he has played more than any other. Certainly that and the album's title track *Born to Run* are two songs I continue to love. The energy, the vision, the images. The Alarm sang about the *Spirit of '76* on their second album *Strength*. It's a song which looks back to those days of youth and dreams and plans and visions. Those *Thunder Road* days.

It's hard to know what I have played the most. *Stay Free* perhaps. Though there are plenty of other go-to tracks. Toploader's *Dancing in the Moonlight* always makes me feel good, as does Chumbawamba's *Tubthumping* and James's *Sit Down*. My favourite numbers are often full-blooded, stomping greats.

They say the music you love at sixteen you love forever. It's true in my case. And any new stuff that emerges is instinctively rated against the likes of *Oliver's Army, Teenage Kicks, Hit Me With Your Rhythm Stick, I Fought the Law* and *Down in the Tube Station at Midnight*. But there are so many other great songs. And sixteen may be a defining age but I still love tunes I heard when I was twelve. And twenty-six... and thirty-six... and forty-six... and even fifty-six.

And I've barely gone near the more reflective stuff, like Kate Winslet's sublime and haunting *What If* and of course Kate Bush's towering *Wuthering Heights*, and Bob Seger's rueful *We've Got Tonight*.

If you only check out one song on YouTube from reading this book, go and listen to Kate Winslet. Even if you've already heard it fifty times. Only if you want to, no pressure.

**Five Songs That Still Sneak Into My Head At Times**
*Life Is Too Short Girl* (Sheer Elegance)
*Miss Grace* (The Thymes)
*I Can't Give You Anything* (Cliff Richard)
*When Will I See You Again* (The Three Degrees)

172

*With a Little Luck* (Wings)

**Desert Island Oldies**

Of all those albums I used to have I only now play a select few. *Tusk* by Fleetwood Mac would be among them, I still love *Rumours* but I know it too well. *Parallel Lines* by Blondie, and Billy Joel's *Glass Houses*, both get a look in. From time to time I put on David Bowie's *Scary Monsters (and Super Creeps)*, along with the album that Lindsey Buckingham and Christine McVie recorded in 2017. And most recently Bruce Springsteen's latest *Only the Strong Survive*.

Other than that it's 'best of' collections and playlists. ELO, Queen, The Jam, The Boomtown Rats, Smokie, occasionally The Undertones and Elvis Costello, and a diverse collection of Abba oldies that harks back to that first 1976 greatest hits collection. Even a bit of Showaddywaddy from time to time. And not forgetting my own New Wave and Britpop compilations. What we once called mix tapes.

If ever I was banished to that desert island with eight discs, the Bible, Bill Shaky and a luxury, I'd have a hard time paring down the choices. That said, here we go.

*Dancing in the Moonlight* By Toploader, *Stay Free* and *White Man in Hammersmith Palais* by The Clash, *Love Grows Where My Rosemary Goes* by Edison Lighthouse, *Sweet Talkin' Woman* by ELO, *Heart of Glass* by Blondie, *Jeans On* by David Dundas, *Tubthumping* by Chumbawamba, *Song for Whoever* by The Beautiful South – and now I realise that's nine. Drat.

I realise now that many of those choices are not just about the songs, but the connections and memories that go with them. *Dancing in the Moonlight* takes me back to jumping around at discos at Lee Abbey, where it never really mattered whether you were any good or not. *Stay Free* of course is about those school days with Stefan, *Love Grows Where My Rosemary Goes* is the song that Lynn and I both love (and number one on the day she was born).

Amy now loves *Sweet Talkin' Woman* as much as I do. *Heart of Glass* takes me back to playing it on repeat as dad and I threw darts in our house one night, *Jeans On* is the song we jumped around to so much with Amy, *Tubthumping* is about my very good friend Justin and his wedding disco when we pogoed one last time in beautiful Virginia. And *Song for Whoever* is just so full of ironic, wry lyrics to the catchiest of tunes. And Amy likes that one too.

And there are probably many more. I suppose I could drop The Clash's *White Man in Hammersmith Palais* at a push. Or maybe I could take that ninth song instead of a luxury item, or better still instead of the works of Mr Shaky. The Bible would be brilliant, but I really don't do the Bard I'm afraid. Sincere apologies, I know so many people love his stuff. Perhaps he'll make it big one day. 😊 The works of Dickens might be better for me, I'd have the time to read *A Tale of Two Cities* and all his other four million words. Just a thought.

**Five Singalong Songs (songs you can't shut up to)**
*We Built This City* (Starship)

*Sweet Talkin' Woman* (ELO)
*Starman* (David Bowie)
*Start Me Up* (The Rolling Stones)
*Waterloo Sunset* (The Kinks)

**Fame**

A few years ago I went all radio-friendly and wrote in to a few shows on Radio Two. Simon Mayo used to do a *Homework Sucks* section on his show, and we wrote in on a couple of occasions with questions – Amy had asked why tiredness causes bags under the eyes so I emailed in about that, (it's about pigment and thick skin and blood vessels and wrinkles... something like that).

And we also wondered why some fruits are berries and some currants – blackberries, and blackcurrants and the like. Turns out there are two definitions – the horticultural and the botanical one – the horticultural one is this... a berry is a cluster of lots of seeds whereas a currant has the seeds on the inside – for the botanical one there is this little thing called the great-global-webternet. ☺

I also emailed in to Johnny Walker's *Sounds of the Seventies*, no prizes for guessing why I listen to that show. There is a feature where you can send in your musical memories, so I wrote in about my Queen-loving days and then my emigration to punk. He featured my selection on a show dedicated to punk. Oddly though I completely failed to mention The Clash among my favourites. I think I panicked.

I wrote in to Steve Wright's *Non-stop Oldies* too and got my thirty minutes of fame on there. I requested

*Love Grows Where My Rosemary Goes...* and that very first purchase *The Legend of Xanadu*. Also *Roadrunner* by Jonathan Richman and Billy Ocean's *Love Really Hurts*, an old favourite from those K-Tel compilation days, and *Jeans On* of course. Plus Bob Seger's *We've Got Tonight*, and from that first batch of four collection-sparking singles Dave Edmunds' rock'n'roller, *I Knew the Bride*. There were others on the list I sent in, and no doubt a hefty fistful of New Wave numbers on there, but you only get thirty minutes, not three days.

I was amazed to find myself getting mentioned on these shows, but I also felt oddly exposed. My private side coming out I think. Though I have these radio moments recorded I'm only now listening back to them to see what was played. We were living in Lynton at the time and Johnny Walker gave a really warm shout out about the town and the vehicular railway which takes you down the cliff to Lynmouth.

When I got the call from one of the shows I once again displayed my ineptitude for one-to-one faith sharing, when the researcher asked me about my job. I told her not to freak out, as if I was a spy or something, and then confessed I was a Bible communicator.

I don't know what comes over me, I really don't, it's as if I imagine people will be mortally offended or laugh me out of town or something. I think I invented the phrase 'overthinking it' when it comes to talking about my faith. I wince even now as I type this, but this also gives me the chance to be a bit confessional about it all. And to hopefully bring you a smile, dear reader, about my Frank Spencer approach to evangelism.

**Top ~~Five~~ ~~Six~~ Seven Favourite Ballads**

*We've Got Tonight* (Bob Seger)

*What If* (Kate Winslet)

*Don't Let It Fade Away* (Darts)

*It's All Coming Back to Me Now* (Celine Dion)

*Will You* (Hazel O'Connor)

*How Long Will I Love You* (Ellie Goulding)

*Part of Me, Part of You* (Glenn Frey)

**A few snaps and musical moments from life so far:**

Hearing the B-side of Jasper Carrot's *Funky Moped* at my friend's place, up the road from our house in Cornwall. Some time in the early '70s. It was a cheeky song based on the magic roundabout. Not at all like those five-minute adventures we got on TV before the news.

Dancing badly in my room in Cornwall to the happy Tavares song *Don't Take Away the Music*, their follow up to *Heaven Must Be Missing An Angel*.

Listening to Don Francisco on tape with Dennis in his car in the Valley of Rocks in Lynton. Hearing that great musical storyteller for the first time. And Dennis was so instrumental in my Christian journey, leading me to pray a prayer of commitment that changed things forever.

Hearing *The Way It Is* by Bruce Hornsby and the Range, I was just setting off from Lee Abbey to go on a church mission and Kent, in the car with me, put on

177

this song I'd never heard before. From those first few notes you're hooked and reeled in.

Roaming the Lee Abbey estate with Huey Lewis's album *Fore!* blasting in my ears from a Walkman. Tracks like *The Power of Love* and *Stuck with You*.

Hearing Tracey Chapman's album for the first time in my friend Andy's flat in 1988. *Talking 'Bout a Revolution* and *Behind the Wall* in particular. I went straight out and bought the cassette.

Seeing Marc Bolan sing *Ride a White Swan* in a documentary about his life and career. He was on Top of the Pops I think and riding in on a huge white swan. Not a real one obviously, but he had this incredible look going on, glam superstar written all over him.

Watching the scene in *Truly Madly Deeply* where Alan Rickman and Juliet Stevenson sing *The Sun Ain't Gonna Shine Any More* together. So feelgood. So wonderful. I watched that scene over and over.

Lynn playing me Marc Cohn's album – tracks like *Walking in Memphis*, and the poignant *True Companion*. A track which grows more poignant with each year, as it's about a couple getting older together.

Singing karaoke at Lee Abbey in 2001 to Jilted John's new wave classic *Jilted John*.

The rave I held for my fortieth birthday whilst working at Lee Abbey, and the encouragement afterwards from a friend Jo who had found a new opportunity to dance after giving up a pre-Christian life of clubbing.

Running round the house with Lynn, Amy and our friends at Lee Abbey, out the front door and back in the back door to Abba's *Mamma Mia*. Round and round and round.

The scene in the movie *Sunshine on Leith* where a whole flashmob crowd sing *I'm Gonna Be (500 Miles)*.

Dancing this Christmas just gone (2022) to Lucy's new Abba dancing Wii game. We had our first New Year's Eve party in years, jumping around to songs like *Does Your Mother Know*.

Amy filling the car with Sia's version of *California Dreamin'* as I drove her back to university. I also love Disturbed's version of *The Sound of Silence* but I have no idea when I first came across that.

**Five Songs About Showbiz**
*Life's Been Good* (Joe Walsh)
*City of Stars* (Ryan Gosling & Emma Stone)
*Pearl's a Singer* (Elkie Brooks)
*Super Trouper* (Abba)
*The Load-Out* (Jackson Browne from the album *Running on Empty*)

### Nerdle

These days I keep my pop brain active by doing the daily Heardle quizzes. You get the first few seconds of an old song and have to hazard a guess. You can do Heardles from the '60s, '70s, '80s, '90s and '00s. There's also a Queen Heardle and a Wham/George Michael one. Plus there's one dedicated to The Beatles – called Beadle.

I guess the name Heardle was derived from the daily Wordle quiz, which made me think that if you had to guess at various gone-off milk types that could be called Curdle. And if you had to answer questions on my pedantic fascination with pop music it could be called Nerdle. And if it was about the world at night it could be Nocturdle. And if it was about hand-cracked stringed instruments it could be a Hurdy-gurdle. And if you had to identify various piles of animal droppings it could be called Tur... I'll stop there.

I also listen to Ken Bruce's *Popmaster*, though he's about to move on from Radio Two to Greatest Hits Radio and take *Popmaster* with him. I'd never attempt to enter it though, I think I'd end up doing a Frank Spencer on air, but it's pleasing to tune in and shout at the radio, and get a few things right. That's the good thing about Heardles – you don't have nine million people listening in.

### Hit and Miss

I realised my age recently when we came across the TV quiz *The Hit List*, in which contestants hear snippets of songs and have to guess the title and/or artist. I was astonished to see it had been around for half a dozen series and I'd only just heard of it. It was a bittersweet watch really, great when the tunes were from the '60s, '70s and '80s, but get me past the year 2000 and I'm like a sixty-year-old who hasn't got a clue.

I did love the moment when one contestant, who clearly had lots of musical knowledge and history, heard the first strains of Joe Jackson's *Is She Really Going Out With Him?* and his face lit up. I think mine did too. Now that's what I call music.

**Top ~~Five~~ Seven Billy Joel Favourites**
*It's Still Rock 'n' Roll To Me*
*My Life*
*We Didn't Start the Fire*
*River of Dreams*
*Say Goodbye to Hollywood*
*Piano Man* (another song packed with great lyrics)
*Scenes from an Italian restaurant* (There's a fantastic live version of this from Long island on YouTube)

**A-changing**
As I type this I can hear our daughter Amy preparing food in the kitchen to tracks from Billy Joel's *Glass Houses*. *All for Leyna* is leaking into my office. Perfect. I loved that album along with so much of Billy Joel's output.

I had *It's Still Rock and Roll to Me* on a 7-inch single and played it to death. That was back in 1980, 42 years ago. Music goes around and comes around. Amy has compiled her own compilations of songs from the '70s and '80s that I once bought and recorded and played non-stop.

Only today she was playing a collection of old songs covered by newer artists, including a singular and powerful version of *California Dreamin'* by Sia. There were several rehashed Queen tracks in there, and Boston's *More Than a Feeling*, plus Scouting for Girls doing *Girls Just Wanna Have* Fun and *Everybody Wants to Rule the World.* In this YouTube age everyone can cover anything and can find an audience for it. The songs put on new clothes according to the times, and Amy goes looking for them. Music is a shared language.

No doubt the songs I've mentioned here will live with me forever, and new songs will come along. And new stories too. And whether old or new they'll link us to others. Like musical parables, there to build bridges over the rivers between us.

Although I've spent time reflecting on the past, and how rich it was, I'm not averse to change. I'm a fan really. God is creative and he calls us to join with him and keep moving on. Not for the sake of it, but because the world is a creative place.

Just as Elvis was never going to be Frank Sinatra, and The Beatles were never going to be Elvis, and The Clash were never going to be The Beatles, and Pulp were never going to be The Clash. And The Killers were never going to be Pulp. The times have always been a-changing.

Creativity is a gift, imagination helps us solve problems and find a way forward. God is into the new things. 'Behold I make all things new…' he says in

182

Revelation 21 and 'Don't dwell on the past, I'm doing a new thing...' in Isaiah 43 and 'God's mercies are new every morning...' in Lamentations 3. New. New. New.

God isn't afraid of fresh ground. Or new anything. He doesn't stand still, though I may often try and hold him down. He's that pillar of cloud still moving on, unboxable, moved by the breath of the spirit. And creativity is endless. You will have had conversations today that didn't exist before, you may have sent texts or WhatsApp messages that you have invented today. You just made them up. This sentence is fresh, it didn't exist till I typed it seconds ago. This one is only being typed... right now. It's brand new. Hot off the keyboard.

That's not to say everything we invent, the conversations and ideas and sentences, are positive and uplifting, but perhaps that's why Paul encourages us, in Philippians 4 v 8, to think on those things that are noble and true and honest and just and worth passing on, so we might litter our ideas with stuff that makes the world better, rather than worse.

### Twelve

The world turns and we still only have twelve notes, and yet the music goes on. And without that gift our lives would be poorer. Whether you love opera, classical, Gregorian chant, hip hop, grunge, garage, choral, reggae, rave, disco, ska, punk, funk, rap, Britpop, soul, rock'n'roll, gospel, worship, jazz, rhythm and blues, electronic, cheesy pop, country, folk, indie, ambient, nursery rhymes, musical theatre, baroque, hymns, house, skiffle, pub rock, techno, calypso, metal,

anthems, ballads, easy listening, dance, K-pop, Latin...
or all of the above (sorry if I missed you out, feel free to
scribble on this page).

Whatever your music, may it warm your heart and
feed your mind, and point you to the one who made
music and keeps giving us songs to sing and tunes to
whistle.

### Psalm 150

Praise the LORD!
Praise him in his mighty heaven!
Praise his unequalled greatness!
Praise him with a blast of the saxophone and trumpet;
praise him with the drum and bass!
Praise him with hip hop and harmonica;
Praise him with acoustic and electric guitars!
Praise him with the keyboard and synth;
praise him with those loud crashing cymbals!
Praise him with lead and backing vocals,
Let everything that lives sing praises to the LORD!
Praise the LORD!

### Be Alert, Be Present

I'll close with this bit of the Bible, from The Message
translation. Although I've spent this book looking back,
here's a great call to not get ensnared by the old. And it
begins with an imaginative and visceral image of the
God who can overcome the most powerful enemies, in
this case the Egyptians. It also paints a wonderful
picture of talking animals!

This is what God says, the God who builds a road right through the ocean, who carves a path through pounding waves, the God who summons horses and chariots and armies – they lie down and then can't get up; they're snuffed out like so many candles: "Forget about what's happened; don't keep going over old history. Be alert, be present. I'm about to do something brand-new. It's bursting out! Don't you see it? There it is! I'm making a road through the desert, rivers in the badlands. Wild animals will say 'Thank you!' – the coyotes and the buzzards. Because I provided water in the desert, rivers through the sunbaked earth, drinking water for the people I chose, the people I made especially for myself, a people custom-made to praise me."

Isaiah 43 v 18-19
From The Message

## An A-Z of Songs Not Mentioned Before Now

*After the Love Has Gone* (Earth Wind and Fire)
*Bang Bang* (BA Robertson)
*Concrete and Clay* (Randy Edelman)
*Dance Away* (Roxy Music)
*Every Little Thing She Does is Magic* (The Police)
*Fantastic Day* (Haircut 100)
*Goodbye Girl* (Squeeze)
*Happy Days* (Pratt & McClain)
*I Heard It Through the Grapevine* (Marvin Gaye)
*Jimmy Jimmy* (The Undertones)
*Kissing in the Back Row of the Movies* (The Drifters)
*Living in a Box* (Living in a Box)
*Maria* (Blondie)
*Never Gonna Give You Up* (Rick Astley)
*One Call Away* (Charlie Puth)
*Promises* (Eric Clapton)
*Queen of Hearts* (Dave Edmunds)
*Rubber Bullets* (10cc)
*Sherry Darling* (Oasis)
*Twist and Shout* (The Beatles)
*Under the Boardwalk* (The Drifters)
*Valerie* (The Zutons)
*Wonderful World* (Sam Cooke)
*X Offender* (Blondie)
*Yesterday* (The Beatles)
*Zombie* (The Cranberries)

A final bit of space for any thoughts, doodlings, scribblings, top fives, or musical memories of your own.